£3.95

Critical Social Studies

Editors: JOCK YOUNG and PAUL WALTON

The contemporary world projects a perplexing picture of political, social and economic upheaval. In these challenging times the conventional wisdoms of orthodox social thought whether it be sociology, economics or cultural studies become inadequate. This series focuses on this intellectual crisis, selecting authors whose work seeks to transcend the limitations of conventional discourse. Its tone is scholarly rather than polemical, in the belief that significant theoretical work is needed to clear the way for a genuine transformation of the existing social order.

Because of this, the series relates closely to recent developments in social thought, particularly to critical theory and neo-Marxism – the emerging European tradition. In terms of specific topics, key pivotal areas of debate have been selected, for example mass culture, inflation, problems of sexuality and the family, the nature of the capitalist state, natural science and ideology. The scope of analysis is broad: the series attempts to break the existing arbitrary divisions between the social-studies disciplines. Its aim is to provide a platform for critical social thought (at a level quite accessible to students) to enter into the major theoretical controversies of the decade.

Other books in the series

PUBLISHED

Trade Unions and the Media
Peter Beharrell and Greg Philo (eds)

Beyond the Sociology of Conflict
David Binns

A Theory of Semiotics
Umberto Eco

Capitalism in Crisis: Inflation and the State
Andrew Gamble and Paul Walton

The Dialectic of Ideology and Technology
Alvin W. Gouldner

Policing the Crisis
Stuart Hall, Chas Critcher, Tony Jefferson,
John Clarke and Brian Roberts

The Political Economy of Science
Hilary Rose and Steven Rose (eds)

The Radicalisation of Science
Hilary Rose and Steven Rose (eds)

FORTHCOMING

The Politics of Decline
Andrew Gamble

Reproducing Ideologies
Stuart Hall

The Multinationals
Richard Kronish

Theories of Underdevelopment
Ian Roxborough

A Textbook of Film
Brian Winston and Colin Young

The State in Capitalist Formations
Howard Wolpe

Media as Myth
Jock Young

INTELLECTUAL AND MANUAL LABOUR

A CRITIQUE OF EPISTEMOLOGY

Alfred Sohn-Rethel

M

© Alfred Sohn-Rethel 1978

First published 1978 by
THE MACMILLAN PRESS LTD
London and Basingstoke
Associated companies in Delhi Dublin
Hong Kong Johannesburg Lagos Melbourne
New York Singapore and Tokyo

Printed in Great Britain by
LOWE AND BRYDONE PRINTERS LTD
Thetford, Norfolk

British Library Cataloguing in Publication Data

Sohn-Rethel, Alfred
    Intellectual and manual labour. – (Critical social Studies).
    1. Knowledge, Theory of   2. Marxian economics
    I. Title   II. Sohn-Rethel, Martin   III. Series
    121   BD163

ISBN 0-333-23045-0
ISBN 0-333-23046-9   Pbk

Contents

Translator's Foreword   ix

Preface   xi

Introduction   1

    PART I Critique of Philosophical Epistemology

1   The Fetishism of Intellectual Labour   13
2   Can there be Abstraction other than by Thought?   17
3   The Commodity Abstraction   19
4   The Phenomenon of the Exchange Abstraction   22
5   Economics and Knowledge   29
6   The Analysis of the Exchange Abstraction   35
    (a) Stating the Question   35
    (b) Practical Solipsism   39
    (c) The Form of Exchangeability of Commodities   43
    (d) Abstract Quantity and the Postulate of
        the Exchange Equation   46
    (e) Abstract Time and Space   48
    (f) The Concept of Value   49
    (g) Substance and Accidents   52
    (h) Atomicity   53
    (i) Abstract Movement   53
    (j) Strict Causality   54
    (k) Concluding Remarks to the Analysis   56
7   The Evolution of Coined Money   58
8   Conversion of the Real Abstraction into the Conceptual Abstraction 60
9   The Independent Intellect   67
    (a) Self-alienation and Self-direction   67
    (b) The Relational Shift   68
    (c) Conversion *post festum* of Exchange   70

(d) Division of Society and Nature 71
(e) Reification at the Root of the Intellect 72
(f) Knowledge from Sources other than Manual
Labour 73
(g) Laws of Nature 74
(h) The Guide-line of Historical Materialism 75
(i) Money as a Mirror of Reflection 76
(j) The Social Form of Thinking 76
(k) The Social Synthesis as the Foundation
of Science 78

PART II Social Synthesis and Production

10 Societies of Production and Societies of Appropriation 83
11 Head and Hand in Labour 84
12 The Beginnings of Surplus Production and
Exploitation 86
13 Head and Hand in the Bronze Age 88
14 The Classical Society of Appropriation 94
15 Mathematics, the Dividing-line of Intellectual
and Manual Labour 101
16 Head and Hand in Medieval Peasant and Artisan
Production 104
17 The Forms of Transition from Artisanry to Science 111
18 The Capitalist Relations of Production 117
19 Galilean Science and the Dynamic Concept of
Inertia 123
20 Bourgeois Science 132

PART III The Dual Economics of Advanced Capitalism

21 From De-socialised to Re-socialised Labour 139
22 A Third Stage of the Capitalist Mode of Production? 140
23 The Turn to Monopoly Capitalism 144
24 Imperialism and Scientific Management 145
25 The Economy of Time and 'Scientific Management' 148
26 The Essentials of Taylorism 149

27 Critique of Taylorism   153
28 The Foundation of Flow Production   159
29 The Unity of Measurement of Man and Machine   161
30 The Dual Economics of Monopoly Capitalism   163
31 The Necessity for a Commensuration of Labour   166
32 The Commensuration of Labour in Action   170
33 The Way to Automation   172
34 The Curse of the Second-Nature   175
35 The Epoch of Transition   178
36 Logic of Appropriation and Logic of Production   180

PART IV Historical Materialism as Methodological
Postulate

37 The Theory of Reflection and its Incompatibilities
    as a Theory of Science   189
38 Materialism versus Empiricism   193
39 Marx's Own Object Lesson   194
40 Necessary False Consciousness   196
41 The Philosophical Issue   199
42 The Essentially Critical Power of Historical Mat-
    erialism   201

Notes and References   205

Books and Articles by Alfred Sohn-Rethel   213

Index   215

Translator's Foreword

Increasingly, those with concern for the future of science – in the final resort, all of us – have to watch helplessly as its course is plotted ever further away from our control. The results of 'man's mastery of nature' are effectively concealed from us. Although official and surreptitious propaganda make claims to the contrary we are quite unable to confirm these claims and often end by resignedly accepting them.

However, some of the most concerned people have begun to look behind the curtain shrouding technology and, in the horror at the travesties it conceals, search desperately for some means to tear it down. A brick hurled through the window of some nuclear research establishment? . . . or, more effective perhaps, a home-made bomb? It is all too plain that these are totally unavailing protests, for the march of science will go on unabated, celebrated in trade agreements worth millions of pounds – for example, the Federal German trade agreement of 1975 to supply Brazil with 40 billion marks' worth of atomic stations by 1990.

By now, science and technology have gained such an ascendency over the common man's understanding that his mere uncomprehending anger can in no way hold them in check. And yet it is supposedly to reproduce him and his labour that this technology has been developed. This is now nothing but a blatant fiction. We know the real motive power behind it is the maximisation of power and profit. It has become clear beyond question that the heads which plot the path of technology and the hands which operate it and which should benefit from it have undergone the most total schism.

When did this schism first occur? Without any clue to its origin the opponent of rampant technology can only rant and rave; he is ill equipped to envisage any remedy. But how can he set out to trace this alienation, this division of head and hand back to its real point of historical departure? How can he begin to unravel the tangled web of relations between man and machine, between society and science, which now threatens to strangle him?

This book attempts to do just that. But in doing so it has of necessity to deal with matters of exasperating abstractness; it has of necessity to delve into areas of such unaccustomed complexity that it might seem all too easy to lose sight of the crucial issues which give rise to the book in the first place. I say 'of necessity' because it is precisely the abstractness and complexity with which the core of the schism is lodged in its historical roots that make us so blind to the overall pattern of perversion traced by technology today. The whole transaction, as it were, has been completed behind our own and our ancestors' backs.

Thus the difficulties of the book are no mere adjuncts but are inherently essential to achieve a truly cogent analysis, in historical materialist terms, of the split between head and hand and of the emergence of abstract thought. The development of modern science and technology has everything to do with these phenomena and until their historical secrets are unravelled before our very eyes technology will continue to ride rough-shod over us.

We ask the reader to be clear what is at stake. If he is, the unavoidable difficulties of the analysis will surely fall into perspective and instead of presenting insurmountable barriers to the book's conclusions will give the key to their proper understanding. But it takes an infinitely deeper theoretical effort to dispel the fetishism of the intellect than it does to continue its worship. This is the use of theory we know from Marx: its use in the service of practice.

MARTIN SOHN-RETHEL

Preface

This enquiry is concerned with the relationship between base and superstructure in the Marxian sense. This, to a large extent, leads into new territory. Marx and Engels have clarified the general architecture of history consisting of productive forces and production relations which together form the material basis for consciousness as superstructure. But they have not left us a blueprint for the staircase that should lead from the base to the superstructure. And it is this with which we are concerned, or at least with its barest scaffolding of formal precision. To continue with our metaphor, the staircase must be given a firm anchorage in the basement, and this, for commodity-producing societies, can only be found in the formal analysis of commodity itself. This analysis, however, requires considerable enlargement and deepening before it can carry the full weight I intend to place on it. For Marx it served to carry the critique of political economy. For us it must carry in addition the critique of the traditional theories of science and cognition.

What is new and bewildering in the present undertaking is that it must lay hand upon the commodity analysis as we have it from Marx, and thus upon that part of his theory commonly regarded as the untouchable foundation stone. It may therefore not be amiss to preface the theoretical presentation with a short sketch of 'thought-biography' to show how the deviating offshoot originated and has taken shape. Moreover it may also be necessary to explain why the investigation has taken fifty years to mature before reaching the light of day.

It began towards the end of the First World War and in its aftermath, at a time when the German proletarian revolution should have occurred and tragically failed. This period led me into personal contact with Ernst Bloch, Walter Benjamin, Max Horkheimer, Siegfried Kracauer and Theodor W. Adorno and the writings of Georg Lukacs and Herbert Marcuse. Strange though it may sound I do not hesitate to say that the new development of Marxist thought which these people represent evolved as the theoretical and ideological superstructure of the revolution that never happened. In it re-echo the thunder of the gun battle for the Marstall in Berlin at Christmas 1918, and the shooting of the Spartacus rising in the following winter. The paradoxical condition of this ideological movement may help to explain its almost exclusive preoccupation with superstructural questions, and the conspicuous lack of concern for the material and economic base that should have been underlying it. As far as I was concerned, though not a member of the Spartacus movement, I was stirred by the political events, partaking in the discussions at street-corners and public meeting-halls, lying under window-sills while bullets pierced the windows – experiences which are traced in the pages to follow.

My political awakening started in 1916, at the age of 17 and still at school, when I began reading August Bebel and Marx. I was thrown out of home and was part of the beginning of the anti-war rebellion of students in my first university year at Heidelberg in 1917, with Ernst Toller as a leading figure. For us the world could have fallen to pieces if only Marx remained intact. But then everything went wrong. The Revolution moved forward and backward and finally ebbed away. Lenin's Russia receded further and further into the distance. At university we learned that even in Marx there were theoretical flaws, that marginal utility economics had rather more in its favour and that Max Weber had successfully contrived sociological antidotes against the giant adversary Marx. But this teaching only made itself felt within the academic walls. Outside there were livelier spirits about, among them my unforgettable friend Alfred Seidel, who in 1924 committed suicide.[1] Here, outside the university, the end of the truth had not yet come.

I glued myself to Marx and began in earnest to read *Capital*, with a relentless determination not to let go. 'Lire le Capital' as Louis Althusser says so rightly! It must have taken some two years when in the background of my university studies I scribbled mountains of paper, seizing upon every one of the vital terms occurring in the first sixty pages of *Capital*, turning them round and round for definitions, and above all for metaphorical significance, taking them to pieces and putting them together

again. And what resulted from this exercise was the unshakeable
certainty of the penetrating truth of Marxist thinking, combined
with an equally unshakeable doubt about the theoretical
consistency of the commodity analysis as it stood. There were
more and other things in it than Marx had succeeded in
reaching! And finally, with an effort of concentration bordering
on madness, it came upon me that in the innermost core of the
commodity structure there was to be found the 'transcendental
subject'. Without need to say so, it was obvious to everybody that
this was sheer lunacy, and no one was squeamish about telling
me so! But I knew that I had grasped the beginning of a thread
whose end was not yet in sight. But the secret identity of
commodity form and thought form which I had glimpsed was so
hidden within the bourgeois world that my first naïve attempts to
make others see it only had the result that I was given up as a
hopeless case. 'Sohn-Rethel is crazy!' was the regretful and final
verdict of my tutor Alfred Weber (brother of Max), who had had
a high opinion of me.

In these circumstances there was of course no hope of an
academic career either, with the consequence that I remained an
outsider all my life with my *idée fixe*. Only a few isolated spirits,
outsiders like myself, had kindred ideas in their minds, and none
more sympathetically so than Adorno, who in his own manner
was on the same track. We checked up on this together in 1936.
He in his whole mental make-up was occupied with completely
different matters rather than the analysis of commodity and
economics. Therefore even my contact with him was only partial
and I was thrown back on my own resources for unravelling my
thread of truth.

That this process was full of deadlocks and long periods of
interruptions, both for reasons of money-earning and because of
other difficulties, goes without saying. The interruptions, periods
of complete recession, add up to even longer durations than the
periods of theoretical work.

The time between 1924 and 1927 was spent in Italy, mainly in
Capri where Benjamin and Bloch were staying; then to Davos for
an international university course, where I met Heidegger, Ernst
Cassirer, Alexander Koyré and others, but had to remain for two
and a half years for a cure of tuberculosis. When I returned to
Germany to face the slump, with absolutely no financial

resources, I was lucky to find work in an office of big business in Berlin.[2]

There I was also engaged in illegal anti-Nazi activities, escaping from arrest by the Gestapo to reach England in 1937. In Birmingham I met Professor George Thomson, the only other man I have known who had also recognised the interconnection of philosophy and money, although in a completely different field from my own – in ancient Greece. I finally finished a long manuscript, 'Intellectual and Manual Labour', in 1951, which, despite strenuous efforts by Thomson and Bernal, was turned down by the publishers Lawrence & Wishart as being too unorthodox for them, and by bourgeois publishers as being too militantly Marxist!

Until 1970 only three small texts of mine were published.[3] Since 1970 several of my books have appeared in Germany (see p. 213), as a result of which I was appointed Guest Professor at the University of Bremen from 1972 to 1976.

For the present English version of this book I am particularly indebted to Dr Wilfried van der Will for reading my script and for his unstinting advice and critical comment; also to my son Martin for his work as translator, and to the late Sigurd Zienau for stimulating discussions during many years of friendship.

My inextinguishable gratitude is due to Joan, my wife, for her untiring effort and unflagging devotion to my work, which has become ours in common.

ALFRED SOHN-RETHEL

Introduction

Our epoch is widely regarded as 'the Age of Science'. Indeed science, and especially scientific technology, exerts an influence upon production and through production upon the economics and the class relations of society. The effects of this have thrown into disarray the historical expectations and conceptions of people convinced of the need for socialism. We are no longer sure of our most trusted ideas of 'scientific socialism' or of our theoretical image of capitalism. How is the progressive destruction of money through inflation in accord with the labour law of value? Are the profits of multinational corporations in keeping with the mechanics of surplus-value? What are the social implications and economics of a technology which tends to absorb the work of human labour? Does this technology widen or narrow the gulf between mental and manual labour? Does it help or hinder a socialist revolution? How does the profit and loss account on the balance sheets of capital relate to the balance between man and nature? Is modern technology class-neutral? Is modern science class-biased?

Has Marxist analysis kept up with the changes of society we have witnessed since the two World Wars? Our insights must reach sufficiently deep to enable us to understand our modern world in Marxist terms and guide our revolutionary practice. Historical materialism was conceived by Marx as the method of the scientific understanding of history. No other position can offer an alternative.

The present study has been undertaken in the belief that an extension to Marxist theory is needed for a fuller understanding of our own epoch. Far from moving away from Marxism this should lead deeper into it. The reason why many essential questions of today cause such difficulties is that our thinking is not Marxist enough – it leaves important areas unexplored.

We understand 'our epoch' as that in which the transition from capitalism to socialism and the building of a socialist society are the order of the day. In contrast, Marx's epoch was engaged in the capitalist process of development; its theoretical perspective was limited to the trends pushing this development to its limits.

It is clear that this change of historical scenery shifts the Marxist field of vision in a significant way. The transition from capitalism to socialism means, according to Marx, 'the ending of pre-history' – the transition from the uncontrolled to the fully conscious development of mankind. To understand society in its final capitalist phase one needs a precise insight into the causality and interrelationships between the growth of the material productive forces and the social relations of production. Marx's *Capital* certainly contains countless references to the mental superstructure determined by the social basis and also to the indispensable intellectual foundations of production, but the problem of the formation of consciousness is not the primary concern of Marx's main work. In our epoch, however, it has assumed crucial importance.

We speak of these intellectual foundations because a historical materialist insight into present-day technology and its scientific basis is essential for the possibility of a consciously organised society. In fact Marx did not focus his attention on a historical-materialist understanding of natural science. In the famous methodological guide-lines of 1859 science is not mentioned as part of the mental superstructure, but it should indeed provide the guide-line for a standpoint of thinking which is itself scientific. Marx saw his own viewpoint as historically conditioned and as anchored in the labour theory of value; it is scientific because it corresponds to the standpoint of the proletariat. But natural science was not given a place as either belonging to the ideological superstructure or the social base. The references to science in *Capital* appear to take their intrinsic methodological possibilities for granted. The historical-materialist omission of the enquiry into the conceptual foundation of science has lead to a schism of thought within the contemporary Marxist camp.

On the one hand, all phenomena contained in the world of consciousness, whether past, present or future, are understood historically as time-bound and dialetic. On the other hand, questions of logic, mathematics and science are seen as ruled by timeless standards. Is a Marxist thus a materialist as far as historical truth is concerned but an idealist when confronted by the truth of nature? Is his thought split between two concepts of truth: the one dialectical and time-bound, the other undialectical, consigning any awareness of historical time to oblivion?

That Marx's own thinking was not rent by any such incompatibilities goes without saying. Extensive proof is found in his early writings, and in the *Communist Manifesto*. Particularly illuminating are the references to the sciences in the *Economic and Philosophic Manuscripts of 1844* (p. 111),[1] which prove that in his historical-materialist conception the sciences were originally included. The relevant evidence and arguments are contained in Alfred Schmidt's outstanding study *The Concept of Nature in the Theory of Marx*.[2]

Even in the Foreword of the first edition of *Capital* Marx calls the 'evolution of the economic formation . . . a process of natural history' and he explains that his own method of approach is calculated to bring out the truth of this statement. But he did not clarify the issue sufficiently to prevent the thought of his successors and followers splitting into two contradictory concepts of truth. Whether the split is overcome or not is vital for the modern theory and practice of socialism. The creation of socialism demands that society makes modern developments of science and technology subservient to its needs. If, on the other hand, science and technology elude historical-materialist understanding, mankind might go, not the way of socialism, but that of technocracy; society would not rule over technology but technology over society, and this not only applies to the western world where technocratic thought is based on positivism;[3] it is no less true of some socialist countries which revere technocracy in the name of 'dialectical materialism'. Thus a historical-materialist explanation of the origins of scientific thought and its development is one of the areas by which Marxist theory should be extended.

There is furthermore a lack of a theory of intellectual and manual labour, of their historical division and the conditions for their possible reunification. In the 'Critique of the Gotha Programme' Marx makes reference to this antithesis that a 'higher phase of communist society' becomes possible only 'after the enslaving subordination of individuals under division of labour, and therewith also the antithesis between mental and physical labour, has vanished'.[4] But before understanding how this antithesis can be removed it is necessary to understand why it arose in the first place.

Clearly the division between the labour of head and hand stretches in one form or another throughout the whole history of class society and economic exploitation. It is one of the phenomena of alienation on which exploitation feeds. Nevertheless, it is by no means self-apparent how a ruling class invariably has at its command the specific form of mental labour which it requires. And although by its roots it is obviously bound up with the conditions underlying the class rule the mental labour of a particular epoch does require a certain independence to be of use to the ruling class. Nor are the bearers of the mental labour, be they priests, philosophers or scientists, the main beneficiaries of the rule to which they contribute; they remain its servants. The objective value of their function, and even the standard of truth itself, emerge in history in the course of the division of head and hand which in its turn is part of the class rule. Thus objective truth and its class function are connected at their very roots and it is only if they can be seen thus linked, logically and historically, that they can be explained. But what implications does this have for the possibility of a modern, classless and yet highly technological society?

This question leads on to the need for a further extension of Marxist theory which did not arise at an earlier epoch: what is in fact the effective line of differentiation between a class society and a classless one? They are both forms of social production relations but this general concept does not convey the difference on which depends the transition from capitalism to socialism, and the varying shades of socialism. What is needed is a specific and unambiguous criterion of social structure, not of ideology, by which a classless society should be recognisable as essentially different from all class societies.

The three groups of questions raised here stand in an inner relationship to each other. The link connecting them is the *social synthesis*: the network of relations by which society forms a coherent whole. It is around this notion that the major arguments of this book will revolve. As social forms develop and change, so also does the synthesis which holds together the multiplicity of links operating between men according to the division of labour.

Every society made up of a plurality of individuals is a network coming into effect through their actions. How they *act* is of primary importance for the social network; what they *think* is of secondary importance. Their activities must interrelate in order to fit into a society, and must contain at least a minimum of uniformity if the society is to function as a whole. This coherence can be conscious or unconscious but exist it must – otherwise society would cease to be viable and the individuals would come to grief as a result of their multiple dependencies upon one another. Expressed in very general terms this is a precondition for the survival of every kind of society; it formulates what I term 'social synthesis'. This notion is thus nothing other than a constituent part of the Marxian concept of 'social formation', a part which, in the course of my long preoccupation with historical forms of thinking, has become indispensable to my understanding of man's social condition. From this observation I derive the general epistemological proposition that the socially necessary forms of thinking of an epoch are those in conformity with the socially synthetic functions of that epoch.

It will, I think, help the reader's comprehension of the somewhat intricate investigation contained in this book if I give a broad outline of the underlying conception.

'It is not the consciousness of men that determine their being, but, on the contrary, their social being that determines their consciousness.' This statement of Marx is not meant as the pronouncement of an intrinsic truth, but is part of the précis of general methodological tenets characteristic of the materialistic conception of history given in the Preface of 1859.[5] This précis indicates *how* the determination of men's consciousness by their social being can be established in any particular instance. My investigation is in strict keeping with the Marxian outline. But, while in that outline the reference is to 'the legal, political, religious, aesthetic or philosophical – in short, ideological forms' in which men become conscious of their social conflicts and fight them out, my preoccupation is with the conceptual foundations of the cognitive faculty *vis-à-vis* nature which in one form or another is characteristic of the ages of commodity production from their beginnings in ancient Greece to the present day. It is for this purpose that I deem it useful to interpret the Marxian concept of 'social being' in accordance with my notion of the 'social synthesis'. This will depend, of course, on how it justifies itself as a methodologically fruitful concept.

In societies based on commodity production the social synthesis is centred on the functions of money as the 'universal equivalent', to use Marx's expression.[6] In this capacity money must be vested with an abstractness of the highest level to enable it to serve as the equivalent to every kind of commodity that may appear on the market. This abstractness of money does not appear as such and cannot be expected to 'appear' as it consists of nothing but form – pure abstract form arising from the disregard of the use-value of the commodities operated by the act of exchange equating the commodities as values. That which constitutes the appearance of money is its material, its shape and size, and the symbols stamped on it; in short, all that makes money into a thing that can be carried about, spent and received. But that which makes this thing 'money' in the sense of value and of equivalence is of a quality radically different from all the properties that can be seen or felt or counted or otherwise perceived. The human labour that has gone into the production of the thing serving as money and into the commodities it serves to exchange determines the magnitude of their value, the proportion in which they are exchanged. But to be labour products is not a property which accrues to the commodities and to money in the relationship of exchange where the abstraction arises. The abstraction does not spring from labour but from exchange as a particular mode of social interrelationship, and it is through exchange that the abstraction imparts itself to labour, making it 'abstract human labour'. The money abstraction can be more properly termed 'the exchange abstraction'.

The peculiar thesis, then, argued on the following pages is to the effect that (1) commodity exchange owes its socially synthetic function to an abstraction which it originates, (2) that this abstraction is not of one piece but is a composite of several elements, (3) that these elementary parts of the abstraction can be separately defined, and (4) that, if this is done in sufficient detail, these constituent elements of the exchange abstraction unmistakably resemble the conceptual elements of the cognitive faculty emerging with the growth of commodity production. As conceptual elements these forms are principles of thought basic to Greek philosophy as well as to modern natural science. In this intellectual capacity they can be labelled by the convenient Kantian term of 'categories *a priori*', especially as this can all the more drastically contrast our materialist account of the categories with the idealistic one of Kant.[7] Additional argumentation will attempt to show that not only analogy but true identity exists between the formal elements of the social synthesis and the formal constituents of cognition. We should then be entitled to state that the conceptual basis of cognition is logically and historically conditioned by the basic formation of the social synthesis of its epoch.

Our explanation thus argues that the categories are historical by origin and social by nature. For they themselves effect the social synthesis on the basis of commodity production in such a way that the cognitive faculty they articulate is an *a priori* social capacity of the mind; although it bears the exactly contrary appearance, that of obeying the principle of *ego cogito*. Kant was right in his belief that the basic constituents of our form of cognition are preformed and issue from a prior origin, but he was wrong in attributing this preformation to the mind itself engaged in the phantasmagorical performance of 'transcendental synthesis *a priori*', locatable neither in time nor in place. In a purely formal way Kant's transcendental subject shows features of striking likeness to the exchange abstraction in its distillation as money: first of all in its 'originally synthetic' character but also in its unique oneness, for the multiplicity of existing currencies cannot undo the essential oneness of their monetary function.

There can be little doubt, then, that the historical-materialist explanation adopted here satisfies the formal exigencies of a theory of cognition. It accounts for the historical emergence of the clear-cut division of intellectual and manual labour associated with commodity production. And by accounting for its genesis it should also help us in perceiving the preconditions of its historical disappearance and hence of socialism as the road to a classless society. As for Kant's idealistic construction, and that of his followers, it becomes clear that they serve to present the division of head and hand as a transcendental necessity.

If this thesis can be argued convincingly it would dispose of the age-old idea that abstraction is the exclusive privilege of thought; the mind would no longer be enshrined in its own immanence. It would give room for a completely different appreciation of science and of mental labour generally laying all intellectual activity open for an understanding of it in terms of the social formation of its epoch and critically evaluating its conceptual structure as well as its functional application in the light of the pertinent social conspectus.

It is clear, on the other hand, that a thesis of this nature cannot draw on factual evidence for its verification but must rely primarily on arguments of reason. So also does the Marxian theory of value and of surplus-value. The facts of history tell in its favour only when viewed in the light of the categories established by the Marxian analysis of the conditions that endow them with the historical reality of valid facts. Our theory is directly concerned only with questions of form, form of consciousness and form of social being, attempting to find their inner connection, a connection which, in turn, affects our understanding of human history. The pivot of the argument lies with the structural form of social being, or, more precisely, with the formal characteristics attaching to commodity production and to the social synthesis arising from it. Thus the Marxian critique of political economy and our critique of bourgeois epistemology are linked by sharing the same methodological foundation: the analysis of the commodity in the opening chapters of *Capital* and, prior to it, in the 'Contribution to the Critique of Political Economy' of 1859. And the salient point of the argument is that this link is one of formal identity. Nevertheless, the difference in scope implies differences in the procedure of the analysis which amount to more than mere shifts of emphasis.

Marx was the first to discover the 'commodity abstraction' at the root of the economic category of value and he analysed it from the twofold viewpoint of form and of magnitude. 'The exchange process gives to the commodity, which it transforms to money, not its value, but its specific form of value', he states in the chapter on 'Exchange'. The form and the magnitude of value spring from different sources, the one from exchange, the other from labour. The critique of political economy hinges upon the understanding of how they combine to become the 'abstract human labour' constituting at once the form and the substance of value. Thus the commodity abstraction or, as we would say, the exchange abstraction is interpreted by Marx foremost as being the 'value abstraction' without involving the need to explore in any detail the source from which the abstraction springs. This is in perfect keeping with Marx's purpose of a critique of political economy. For our purpose, however, we must concentrate in the first place on the formal aspect of value, not only in preference to, but even in separation from its economic content of labour. Or, to put it differently, we have to proceed from the commodity abstraction to the source from where the abstraction emanates and must carry through a painstakingly accurate and detailed analysis of the formal structure of exchange as the basis of its socially synthetic function.

Thus, notwithstanding their common methodological foundation, the critique of political economy and the critique of philosophical epistemology have to pursue their tasks in complete independence of each other, in strict accordance, that is, with the diverse systematic nature of their subject-matters. The fields of economics and of natural science have not a term in common, and it would be a hopeless endeavour to try to cope with the critique of epistemology by grafting it on to the Marxian critique of political economy. It must be undertaken as an investigation standing on its own ground to be judged by its own standards. This does not prevent both these critical pursuits from being inseparably bound up with each other in the results they yield for our understanding of history. The class antagonisms which commodity production engenders in all its stages – in Marx's terms 'the ancient classical, the feudal, and the modern bourgeois modes of production'[8] are intrinsically connected with closely corresponding forms of division of head and hand; but how this connection operates will become recognisable only when the form analysis of the exchange abstraction has been accomplished.

PART I

CRITIQUE OF PHILOSOPHICAL EPISTEMOLOGY

I

The Fetishism of Intellectual Labour

A critique needs a well-defined object at which it is directed; we choose philosophical epistemology. What is the salient feature which marks it as our particular object? Which philosophy most significantly represents it and is most rewarding to criticise? From the Introduction it is clear that our choice has fallen upon the Kantian theory of cognition. This does not, however, mean that the reader must be a specialist in this particularly daunting philosophy – far from it.

Marx clarifies the object of his critique as follows: 'Let me point out once and for all that by classical political economy I mean all the economists who, since the time of W. Petty, have investigated the real internal framework of bourgeois relations of production, as opposed to the vulgar economists. . . .'[1] Classical political economy in the sense of this definition culminated in the work of Adam Smith (1723–90) and David Ricardo (1772–1823) and accordingly the discussion of their theories bulks largest in Marx's critical studies – for instance those collected as 'Theories of Surplus Value'. This does not, however, oblige anyone to embark upon a study of Smith and Ricardo before reading Marx, even though, conversely, it is essential to have read Marx before looking at Smith and Ricardo. Marx's work in economics starts where the peak of bourgeois economics reaches its limits.*

Can we draw any parallel to this framework of the Marxian critique to elucidate our own undertaking in the field of philosophical epistemology? I understand by this name the

---

* In Part IV the reader will find more on the methodological significance of this order of things.

epistomology which since the time of Descartes (1596–1650) seized upon the newly founded natural science of the mathematical and experimental method established by Galileo (1564–1642). Thus we describe philosophical epistemology as the theory of scientific knowledge undertaken with the aim of elaborating a coherent, all-embracing ideology to suit the production relations of bourgeois society. This endeavour culminated in the main works of Kant (1724–1804), especially his *Critique of Pure Reason*.[2] I therefore confine my main attention to Kant's philosophy of science which I consider to be the classical manifestation of the bourgeois fetishism of intellectual labour. Smith and Kant have in common that each is the first to have placed his respective discipline on a systematic foundation. Kant might at his time have been introduced to an English public as the Adam Smith of epistemology, and at the same period Smith could have been recommended to a German audience as the Immanuel Kant of political economy.

However, in the light of Engels's *Ludwig Feuerbach and the Outcome of Classical German Philosophy*[3] and his survey of 'the whole movement since Kant' one might feel inclined to rank Hegel (1770–1831) above Kant, especially since Ricardo is frequently placed on a level with his contemporary, Hegel, in comparison with Smith and Kant. While both the latter, in their own fields, evolved the postulates which a fully fledged bourgeois society should be expected to realise, Ricardo and Hegel, independently of each other, faced up to the inherent contradictions revealed by that society upon the achievement of this realisation, brought about by the advent of the French Revolution of 1789–94 and its Napoleonic aftermath. But there is one important difference which sets Hegel on a plane apart from Ricardo. He discarded the epistemological approach altogether and outstripped the limitations of the critical standards of thinking observed by Kant and adhered to by Ricardo in order to lift himself to the height of 'speculative and absolute idealism'. This gave him free rein to carry philosophy to its consummation, but it makes him unsuited as the object for my own critique.

Many a good Marxist will want to join issue with me on this apparently disparaging treatment of Hegel. For was not Hegel, after all, the discoverer of dialectics and does not Marx accept him as such? 'The mystification which dialectic suffers in Hegel's hands, by no means prevents him from being the first to present its general form of working in a comprehensive and conscious manner. With him it is standing on its head. It must be inverted, in order to discover the rational kernel within the mystical shell.'[4] True, this is what Marx says of Hegel in regard to the dialectic, but some Marxists have joined issue with Marx himself for leaving this vital subject so incompletely elucidated. I must say that I have never felt quite convinced that to advance from the critical idealism of Kant to the critical materialism of Marx the road should necessarily lead via the absolute idealism of Hegel. There should be the possibility of connecting Kant and Marx by a direct route at least systematically which would also yield an understanding of dialectics as the critical, and self-critical, approach without first presenting it in the misleading guise of a system of logic. Nevertheless I admit that the dialectic as evolved by Hegel affords a way of thinking which is infinitely superior to the fixed dualism of Kant. But the complaint about its dualism can affect the Kantian mode of thought only as bourgeois philosophy. And there it does it a service. For the unyielding dualism of this philosophy is surely a more faithful reflection of the realities of capitalism than can be found in the efforts of the illustrious post-Kantians striving to rid themselves of it by drawing all and everything into the redeeming 'immanency of the mind'. How can the truth of the bourgeois world present itself other than as dualism?

Hegel realised that the ideal of the truth could not acquiesce with it as the ultimate state of affairs and he engaged on dialectics as a road transcending the bourgeois limitations. Therein lies his greatness and the importance of the impulse that emanated from the dynamic of this conception. But he could not himself step out of the bourgeois world at his epoch, and so he attained the unity outreaching Kant only by dispensing with the epistemological critique, and hence by way of hypostasis. He did not *make* 'thinking' and 'being' one, and did not enquire how they could be one. He simply argued that the idea of the truth *demands* them to be one, and if logic is to be the logic of the truth it has to start with that unity as its presupposition. But what is the kind of 'being' with which 'thinking' could be hypostatised as one, and their unity be a system of logic? It was nothing more, and nothing more real, than the 'being' implied when I say 'I *am* I', since after all, 'am' is the first person singular of the verb 'to be' in its present tense. And so Hegel starts his dialectics by a process of the mind within the mind. The Hegelian dissolution of the Kantian antitheses is not achieved by dissolving them, but by making them perform as a process. The Hegelian dialectics has no other legitimacy than that it is a process occurring. Questioned as to its possibility it would prove impossible. Adorno was perfectly right in saying: 'If the Hegelian synthesis did work out, it would only be the wrong one.'

When Marx in the last of his *Theses on Feuerbach*[5] wrote: 'The philosophers have only *interpreted* the world in various ways; the point however is to *change* it', Hegel must have been foremost in his thoughts, because in his philosophy the very dialectics of the real change is wasted on merely ontologising 'the Idea'. What else could this Idea be as an outcome of the dialectic as Logic, but the idealisation of the bourgeois world rising to the height of 'thinking' and 'being' embracing each other in the perfection of the bourgeois State as the Prussian paragon of the constitutional monarchy. A similar treatment is meted out to all the spheres to which Hegel extended his speculation, that of the law, the mind, aesthetics, religion, history and even nature. To them all the same pattern of Logic could be made applicable by modifying the kind of 'being' that entered into unity with 'thinking' in each particular field.

I am well aware that stressing only its negative side distorts Hegel's philosophy out of recognition by suppressing the immense wealth and depth of content it owes to the revolutionary impulse of the dialectic. Hegel's is a philosophy which might be said to be wrapped in twilight from beginning to end, and I do not want my few remarks to be misunderstood as being a general condemnation of this outstanding work. My concern is narrowly confined to one question only: the treatment of the Kantian epistemology by Hegel on the one hand and Marx on the other.

Thus it is easy to see what Hegel's interest was in dispensing with the epistemological enquiry of Kant, but it was surely not the Marxian interest to do likewise. The Hegelian motivation was rooted in the mystification of the dialectic which aroused Marx's criticism. Marx's elimination of the Kantian kind of enquiry should not be understood simply as an imitation of Hegel's. Marx must have had his own independent reasons for it, grounded in his materialistic conception of the dialectic, not in the idealistic one of Hegel.

The Kantian enquiry was aimed at an explanation of the phenomenon of the human intellect such as it manifested itself in the mathematical science founded by Galileo and perfected by Newton. What was wrong with Kant's enquiry was that he looked into the nature of the human mind for an answer. Marx could only be satisfied with an answer drawn from natural history and the human departure from it in social and economic developments arising from man's producing his own means of livelihood. This kind of answer could not possibly be gained from Hegel's philosophy. But it is this answer that we have in mind when we suggest a direct cut-through from Kant to Marx by way of a critical liquidation of Kant's enquiry, rather than by purely discarding it.

2

Can there be Abstraction other than by Thought?

Forms of thought and forms of society have one thing in common. They are both 'forms'. The Marxian mode of thought is characterised by a conception of form which distinguishes it from all other schools of thinking. It derives from Hegel, but this only so as to deviate from him again. For Marx, form is time-bound. It originates, dies and changes within time. To conceive of form in this way is characteristic of dialectical thought, but with Hegel, its originator, the genesis and mutation of form is only within the power of the mind. It constitutes the 'science of logic'; form processes in any other field, say nature or history, Hegel conceived only in the pattern of logic. The Hegelian concept of dialectic finally entitles the mind not only to primacy over manual work but endows it with omnipotence.

Marx, on the other hand, understands the time governing the genesis and the mutation of forms as being, from the very first, historical time – the time of natural and of human history.[6] * That is why the form processes cannot be made out in anticipation. No *prima philosophia* under any guise has a place in Marxism. What is to be asserted must first be established by investigation; historical materialism is merely the name for a methodological postulate and even this only became clear to Marx 'as a result of my studies'.

Thus one must not ignore the processes of abstraction at work in the emergence of historical forms of consciousness. Abstraction can be likened to the workshop of conceptual thought and its process must be a materialistic one if the assertion that consciousness is determined by social being is to hold true. A derivation of consciousness from social being presupposes a process of abstraction which is part of this being. Only so can we validate the statement that 'the social being of man determines his consciousness'. But with this point of view the historical materialist stands in irreconcilable opposition to all traditional, theoretical philosophy. For this entire tradition it is an established fact that abstraction is the inherent activity and the exclusive privilege of thought; to speak of abstraction in any other sense is regarded as irresponsible, unless of course one uses the word merely metaphorically. But to acquiesce in this philosophical tradition would preclude the realisation of the postulate of historical materialism. If the formation of the consciousness, by the procedure of abstraction, is exclusively a matter for the consciousness itself, then a chasm opens up between the forms of consciousness on the one side and its alleged determination in being on the other. The historical materialist would deny in theory the existence of this chasm, but in practice has no solution to offer, none at any rate that would bridge the chasm.

Admittedly it must be taken into consideration that the

---

* 'We know only one science, the science of history. History can be regarded from two sides: the history of nature and the history of man. Neither side, however can be separated from time. . . .' (*The German Ideology* (in German: *Frühschriften*, ed. S. Landshut and J. P. Mayer, p. 10).) The paragraph that begins these lines is crossed out in Marx's handwritten manuscript, but they retain their value as an essential expression of his thought.

philosophical tradition is itself a product of the division between mental and manual labour, and since its beginning with Pythagoras, Heraclitus and Parmenides has been a preserve of intellectuals for intellectuals, inaccessible to manual workers. Little has changed here, even today. For this reason the testimony of this tradition, even if unanimous, does not carry the weight of authority for those who take their stand with the manual worker. The view that abstraction was not the exclusive property of the mind, but arises in commodity exchange was first expressed by Marx in the beginning of *Capital* and earlier in the *Critique of Political Economy* of 1859, where he speaks of an abstraction other than that of thought.

3
The Commodity Abstraction

The form of commodity is abstract and abstractness governs its whole orbit. To begin with, exchange-value is itself abstract value in contrast to the use-value of commodities. The exchange-value is subject only to quantitative differentiation, and this quantification is again abstract compared with the quantity which measures use-values. Marx points out with particular emphasis that even labour, when determining the magnitude and substance of value, becomes 'abstract human labour', human labour purely as such. The form in which commodity-value takes on its concrete appearance as money – be it as coinage or bank-notes – is an abstract *thing* which, strictly speaking, is a contradiction in terms. In the form of money riches become abstract riches and, as owner of such riches, man himself becomes an abstract man, a private property-owner. Lastly a society in which commodity exchange forms the *nexus rerum* is a purely abstract set of relations where everything concrete is in private hands.

The essence of commodity abstraction, however, is that it is not thought-induced; it does not originate in men's minds but in their actions. And yet this does not give 'abstraction' a merely metaphorical meaning. It is abstraction in its precise, literal sense. The economic concept of value resulting from it is characterised by a complete absence of quality, a differentiation purely by quantity and by applicability to every kind of commodity and service which can occur on the market. These qualities of the economic value abstraction indeed display a striking similarity with fundamental categories of quantifying natural science without, admittedly, the slightest inner relationship between these heterogeneous spheres being as yet recognisable. While the concepts of natural science are thought abstractions, the economic concept of value is a real one. It exists nowhere other than in the human mind but it does not spring from it. Rather it is purely social in character, arising in the spatio-temporal sphere of human interrelations. It is not people who originate these abstractions but their actions. 'They do this without being aware of it.'[7]

In order to do justice to Marx's *Critique of Political Economy* the commodity or value abstraction revealed in his analysis must be viewed as a *real abstraction* resulting from spatio-temporal activity. Understood in this way, Marx's discovery stands in irreconcilable contradiction to the entire tradition of theoretical philosophy and this contradiction must be brought into the open by *critical confrontation* of the two conflicting standpoints. But such a confrontation does not form part of the Marxian analysis.

I agree with Louis Althusser that in the theoretical foundations of *Capital* more fundamental issues are at stake than those showing in the purely economic argument. Althusser believes that *Capital* is the answer to a question implied but not formulated by Marx.[8] Althusser defeats the purpose of his search for this question by insisting 'que la production de la connaissance . . . constitue un processus qui se passe *tout entier dans la pensée*'. He understands Marx on the commodity abstraction metaphorically, whereas it should be taken literally and its epistemological implications pursued so as to grasp how Marx's method turns Hegel's dialectic 'right side up'. The unproclaimed theme of *Capital* and of the commodity analysis is in fact the real abstraction uncovered there. Its scope reaches further than economics – indeed it concerns the heritage of philosophy far more directly than it concerns political economy.

Some people go further and accuse Marx of having ignored the epistemological implications of his own mode of thinking. Here I agree that, if one takes up these implications and pursues them consistently, epistemology itself undergoes a radical transformation and indeed merges into a theory of society. However I believe that the fallacies of the epistemological and idealistic tradition are more effectively eliminated if one does not talk of 'the theory of knowledge' but the division of mental and manual labour instead. For then the practical significance of the whole enquiry becomes apparent.

If the contradiction between the real abstraction in Marx and the thought abstraction in the theory of knowledge is not brought to any critical confrontation, one must acquiesce with the total lack of connection between the scientific form of thought and the historical social process. Mental and manual labour must remain divided. This means, however, that one must also acquiesce with the persistence of social class division, even if this assumes the form of socialist bureaucratic rule. Marx's omission of the theory of knowledge results in the lack of a theory of mental and manual labour; it is, in other words, the theoretical omission of a precondition of a classless society which was seen by Marx himself to be fundamental.

The political implication heightens its theoretical importance. For not only must the conception of history be broadened to include science, but also its method must be a consistently critical one. For Marx arrives at the correct understanding of things only by critically tracing the causes that give rise to the false consciousness operating in class society.

Thus, to the conditions of a classless society we must add, in agreement with Marx, the unity of mental and manual labour, or as he puts it, the disappearance of their division. And the present study maintains that an adequate insight can only be gained into the conditions of a classless society by investigating the origin of the division of head and hand.

This involves a critique of philosophical epistemology which is the false consciousness arising from this division. The Marxian concept of critique owes its parentage to Kant in his *Critique of Pure Reason*. We now apply in full circle the principle of critique in this sense to the Kantian epistemology. This is the classical manifestation of the bourgeous fetishism embodied in the mental labour of science. We must trace the division of mental and manual labour back to its earliest occurrence in history. This origin we date from the beginnings of Greek philosophy because its antecedents in Egypt and Mesopotamia are prescientific.

Our task, now, amounts to the critical demonstration of the commodity abstraction. This is only a reformulation of what was previously referred to as 'critical confrontation'. We have to prove that the exchange abstraction is, first, a real historical occurrence in time and space, and, second, that it is an abstraction in the strict sense acknowledged in epistemology. This enquiry must be preceded by a description of the phenomenon under investigation.

4

The Phenomenon of the Exchange Abstraction

The Marxist concept of commodity abstraction refers to the labour which is embodied in the commodities and which determines the magnitude of their value. The value-creating labour is termed 'abstract human labour' to differentiate it from concrete labour which creates use-values. Our main concern is to clarify this 'commodity abstraction' and to trace its origin to its roots.

It must be stated from the outset that our analysis of exchange and value differs in certain respects from that of Marx in the opening of volume 1 of *Capital* without, for that matter, contradicting his analysis. Marx was concerned with the 'critique of political economy', while our subject is the theory of scientific knowledge and its historical-materialist critique. However, Marx himself has defined the aspect of exchange as it concerns our purpose:

> However long a series of periodical reproductions and preceding accumulations the capital functioning today may have passed through, it always preserves its original virginity. So long as the laws of exchange are observed in every single act of exchange – taken in isolation – the mode of appropriation [of the surplus – S.-R.] can be completely revolutionised without in any way affecting the property rights which correspond to commodity production. The same rights remain in force both at the outset, when the product belongs to its producer, who, exchanging equivalent for equivalent, can enrich himself only by his own labour, and in the period of capitalism, when social wealth becomes to an ever-increasing degree the property of those who are in a position to appropriate the unpaid labour of others over and over again.[9]

Hence the formal structure of commodity exchange, in every single act, remains the same throughout the various stages of commodity production. I am concerned exclusively with this formal structure, which takes no account of the relationship of value to labour. Indeed where labour is taken into consideration we are in the field of economics. Our interest is confined to the abstraction contained in exchange which we shall find determines the conceptual mode of thinking peculiar to societies based on commodity production.

In order to pursue our particular purpose of tracing to its origin the abstraction permeating commodity exchange we slightly modify the starting base of the analysis. Marx begins by distinguishing use-value and exchange-value as the major contrasting aspects of every commodity. We trace these aspects to the different human activities to which they correspond, the actions of use and the action of exchange. The relationship between these two contrasting kinds of activity, use and exchange, is the basis of the contrast and relationship between use-value and exchange-value. The explanation of the abstraction of exchange is contained in this relationship.

The point is that use and exchange are not only different and contrasting by description, but are mutually exclusive in time. They must take place separately at different times. This is because exchange serves only a change of ownership, a change, that is, in terms of a purely *social status* of the commodities as owned property. In order to make this change possible on a basis of negotiated agreement the physical condition of the commodities, their *material status*, must remain unchanged, or at any rate must be assumed to remain unchanged. Commodity exchange cannot take place as a recognised social institution unless this separation of exchange from use is stringently observed. This is a truth which need only be uttered to be convincing, and I regard it as a firm basis on which to build far-reaching conclusions.

First, therefore, let us be clear as to the specific nature of this particular restriction of use. For there are, of course, countless situations apart from exchange where the use of things is stopped, hindered, interrupted or otherwise disputed. None of these have the same significance as exchange. Things may be stored for later use, others put on one side for the children, wine may be kept in the cellar to mature, injured bodies be ordered a rest, and so on. These are stoppages or delays of use decided upon by the users themselves and done in the service of their use. Whether they happen in a private household or on the wider basis of production carried on in common with other people, cases of this kind are not on a level comparable with exchange, because use here is not forbidden by social command or necessity. But social interference occurs wherever there is exploitation without for that reason alone being necessarily similar to exchange. Long before there was commodity production exploitation assumed one of the many forms of what Marx has termed 'direct lordship and bondage'. This is exploitation based on unilateral appropriation as opposed to the reciprocity of exchange. In ancient Bronze Age Egypt, for instance, priests and scribes and other servants of the Pharaoh were engaged to collect surplus produce from the Nilotic peasants and put it into storage. Once the produce was collected neither the peasant producers nor the collectors had access to these goods for their own use, for the power and authority for the collection emanated from the Pharaoh. There was a transference of property, but a public, not a private, one, and there was the same immutability of the material status of the products held in store for disposal by the ruling authorities which applies in the case of commodities in exchange. There were significant formal similarities between Bronze Age Egypt or Babylonia and Iron Age Greece, and we shall find in the second part of this study that the proto-science which emerged in the ancient oriental civilisations can be accounted for on these grounds. But the great difference is that the social power imposing this control over the use of things was in the nature of the personal authority of the Pharaoh obeyed by every member of the ruling set-up. In an exchange society based on commodity production, however, the social power has lost this personal character and in its place is an anonymous necessity which forces itself upon every individual commodity owner. The whole of the hierarchical superstructure of the Egyptian society has disappeared, and the control over the use and disposal of things is now exercised anarchically by the mechanism of the market in accordance with the laws of private property, which are in fact the laws of *the separation* of exchange and use.

Thus the salient feature of the act of exchange is that its separation from use has assumed the compelling necessity of an objective social law. Wherever commodity exchange takes place, it does so in effective 'abstraction' from use. This is an abstraction not in mind, but in fact. It is a state of affairs prevailing at a definite place and lasting a definite time. It is the state of affairs which reigns on the market.

There, in the market-place and in shop windows, things stand still. They are under the spell of one activity only; to change owners. They stand there waiting to be sold. While they are there for exchange they are there not for use. A commodity marked out at a definite price, for instance, is looked upon as being frozen to absolute immutability throughout the time during which its price remains unaltered. And the spell does not only bind the doings of man. Even nature herself is supposed to abstain from any ravages in the body of this commodity and to hold her breath, as it were, for the sake of this social business of man. Evidently, even the aspect of non-human nature is affected by the banishment of use from the sphere of exchange.

The abstraction from use in no way implies, however, that the use-value of the commodities is of no concern in the market. Quite the contrary. While exchange banishes use from the actions of marketing people, it does not banish it from their minds. However, it must remain confined to their minds, occupying them in their imagination and thoughts only. This is not to say that their thoughts need lack reality. Customers have the right to ascertain the use-value of the commodities on offer. They may examine them at close quarters, touch them, try them out, or try them on, ask to have them demonstrated if the case arises. And the demonstration should be identically like the use for which the commodity is (or is not) acquired. On standards of empiricism no difference should prevail between the use on show and the use in practice. This, however, is the difference that matters on the business standards which rule in the market. Of a commodity in the market the empirical data come under reservations like those argued in subjective idealism; material reality accrues to them when the object is out of the market and passes, by virtue of the money paid, into the private sphere of the acquiring customer.

It is certain that the customers think of commodities as objects of use, or nobody would bother to exchange them (and confidence tricksters would be out of business). The banishment of use during exchange is entirely independent of what the specific use may be and can be kept in the private minds of the exchanging agents (buyers and sellers of sodium chlorate might have gardening in mind or bomb-making).

Thus, in speaking of the abstractness of exchange we must be careful not to apply the term to the consciousness of the exchanging agents. They are supposed to be occupied with the use of the commodities they see, but occupied in their imagination only. It is the action of exchange, and the action alone, that is abstract. The consciousness and the action of the people part company in exchange and go different ways. We have to trace their ways separately, and also their interconnection.

As commodity production develops and becomes the typical form of production, man's imagination grows more and more separate from his actions and becomes increasingly individualised, eventually assuming the dimensions of a private consciousness. This is a phenomenon deriving its origin, not from the private sphere of use, but precisely from the public one of the market. The individualised consciousness also is beset by abstractness, but this is not the abstractness of the act of exchange at its source. For the abstractness of that action cannot be noted when it happens, since it only happens because the consciousness of its agents is taken up with their business and with the empirical appearance of things which pertains to their use. One could say that the abstractness of their action is beyond realisation by the actors because their very consciousness stands in the way. Were the abstractness to catch their minds their action would cease to be exchange and the abstraction would not arise. Nevertheless the abstractness of exchange *does* enter their minds, but only after the event, when they are faced with the completed result of the circulation of the commodities. The chief result is money in which the abstractness assumes a separate embodiment. Then, however, 'the movement through which the process has been mediated vanishes in its own result, leaving no trace behind'.[10] This will occupy us more fully later on. Here we want to return once more to the separation of exchange from use and to its basic nature.

When looking at use and exchange as kinds of human practice it becomes plain to see in what manner they exclude each other. Either can take place only while the other does not. The practice of 'use' covers a well-nigh unlimited field of human activities; in fact it embraces all the material processes by which we live as bodily beings on the bosom of mother earth, so to speak, comprising the entirety of what Marx terms 'man's interchange with nature' in his labour of production and his enjoyment of consumption. This material practice of man is at a standstill, or assumed to be at a standstill, while the other practice, that of exchange, holds sway. This practice has no meaning in terms of nature: it is purely social by its constitution and scope. 'Not an atom of matter enters into the objectivity of commodities as values; in this it is the direct opposite of the coarsely sensuous objectivity of commodities as physical bodies.'[11] The point is that notwithstanding the negation that exchange implies of the physical realities of use and use-value, the transfer of possession negotiated under property laws in no way lacks physical reality itself. Exchange involves the movement of the commodities in time and space from owner to owner and constitutes events of no less physical reality than the activities of use which it rules out. It is indeed precisely because their physical reality is on a par that both kinds of practice, exchange and use, are mutually exclusive in time. It is in its capacity of a real event in time and space that the abstraction applies to exchange, it is in its precise meaning a real abstraction and the 'use' from which the abstraction is made encompasses the entire range of sense reality.

Thus we have, on the basis of commodity production, two spheres of spatio-temporal reality side by side, yet mutually exclusive and of sharply contrasting description. It would help us to have names by which we could designate them. In German the world of 'use' is often called 'the first or primary nature', material in substance, while the sphere of exchange is termed a 'second, purely social, nature' entirely abstract in make-up. They are both called 'nature' to point to the fact that they constitute worlds equally spatio-temporal by reality and inextricably interwoven in our social life. The ancient legend of King Midas, who wished for everything he touched to turn to gold and died upon having his wish fulfilled, vividly illustrates how contrasting in reality and yet how closely associated in our minds both these natures are.

This, in the briefest way, is the foundation on which I shall base my historical and logical explanation of the birth of philosophy in Greek society of slave-labour, and of the birth of modern science in European society based on wage-labour. To substantiate my views three points have to be established: (a) that commodity exchange is an original source of abstraction; (b) that this abstraction contains the formal elements essential for the cognitive faculty of conceptual thinking; (c) that the real abstraction operating in exchange engenders the ideal abstraction basic to Greek philosophy and to modern science.

On the first point, it is necessary to recapitulate the points made so far: commodity exchange is abstract because it excludes use; that is to say, the action of exchange excludes the action of use. But while exchange banishes use from the actions of people, it does not banish it from their minds. The minds of the exchanging agents must be occupied with the purposes which prompt them to perform their deal of exchange. Therefore while it is necessary that their action of exchange should be abstract from use, there is also necessity that their minds should not be. The action alone is abstract. The abstractness of their action will, as a consequence, escape the minds of the people performing it. In exchange, *the action is social, the minds are private*. Thus, the action and the thinking of people part company in exchange and go different ways. In pursuing point (*b*) of our theses we shall take the way of the action of exchange, and this will occupy the next two chapters. For point (*c*) we shall turn to the thinking of the commodity owners and of their philosophical spokesmen, in Part II of the book.

5
Economics and Knowledge

How does society hold together when production is carried out independently by private producers, and all forms of previous production in common have broken asunder? On such a basis society can cohere in no other way than by the buying and selling of the products as commodities. Private production becomes increasingly specialised and the producers become increasingly dependent upon one another according to the division of labour reigning between them. The only solution to their interdependence is commodity exchange.

The nexus of society is established by the network of exchange and by nothing else. It is my buying my coat, not my wearing it, which forms part of the social nexus, just as it is the selling, not the making of it. Therefore, to talk of the social nexus, or, as we may call it, the social synthesis, we have to talk of exchange and not of use. In enforcing the separation from use, or more precisely, from the actions of use, the activities of exchange presuppose the market as a time- and space-bound vacuum devoid of all inter-exchange of man with nature.

What enables commodity exchange to perform its socialising function – to effect the social synthesis – is its abstractness from everything relating to use. Our question could thus also be rephrased in the paradoxical form: how is 'pure' socialisation possible? – the word 'pure' here conforming to the same criteria of 'pureness' which Kant applies to his concept of 'pure mathematics' and 'pure science'. In this wording our question offers a time- and space-bound and historical corollary to the Kantian enquiry into the conditions by which pure mathematics and pure science are possible. Kant's enquiry was an idealistic one. Translated into Marxist terms it reads: How is objective knowledge of nature possible from sources other than manual labour? Formulated in this way our questions aim directly at the pivotal point of the division between mental and manual labour – a division which is a socially necessary condition of the capitalist mode of production.

These remarks should show how our form analysis of the commodity abstraction can serve the historical-materialist critique of the traditional theory of knowledge as a complement to Marx's critique of political economy. This merits further elucidation.

In commodity exchange the action and the consciousness of people go separate ways. Only the action is abstract; the consciousness of the actors is not. The abstractness of their action is hidden to the people performing it. The actions of exchange are reduced to strict uniformity, eliminating the differences of people, commodities, locality and date. The uniformity finds expression in the monetary function of one of the commodities acting as the common denominator to all the others. The relations of exchange transacted in a market express themselves in quantitative differences of this uniform denominator as different 'prices' and create a system of social communication of actions performed by individuals in complete independence of one another and oblivious of the socialising effect involved. The pivot of this mode of socialisation is the abstraction intrinsic to the action of exchange. This abstraction is the dominating form element of commodity exchange to which we give an even wider significance than did Marx, who was the first to discover it.

The chief difference distinguishing the Marxian treatment of economics from the bourgeois one lies in the importance accorded to the formal aspects of economic reality. The understanding of form as attached to being and not only to thinking was the main principle of dialectics which Marx drew from Hegel.

> Political economy has indeed analysed value and its magnitude, however incompletely, and has uncovered the content concealed within these forms. But it has never once asked the question why this content has assumed that particular form, that is to say, why labour is expressed in value, and why the measurement of labour by its duration is expressed in the magnitude of the value of the product.[12]

This Marxian sense of the objective necessity and the anonymity of the formal developments of economic life in its sheer historical reality excels in the analysis of the commodity and of the genesis of its monetary expression.

Thus the difference between the Marxian critique of political economy and our critique of idealistic epistemology cannot be confined to the simple contrast between the economics of the magnitude of values and the formal aspect of value and commodity exchange. Both are inseparably linked in the Marxian analysis. Our interest centres on the conversion of the forms of the social being in the epochs of commodity production into the forms of cognition peculiar to these epochs. Marx clearly indicates the way in which this conversion takes place. The separation of action and consciousness of people engaged in exchange make it impossible for the forms of exchange to impart themselves to the human mind at the source of these forms. The abstraction applying to the mere action of exchange produces its own practical results, the principal one of which is the emergence of money. Marx has analysed this process in great detail in the first chapter of *Capital* and sums it up again as follows:

> The historical broadening and deepening of the phenomenon of exchange develops the opposition between use-value and value which is latent in the nature of the commodity. The need to give an external expression to this opposition for the purposes of commercial intercourse produces the drive towards an independent form of value, which finds neither rest nor peace until an independent form has been achieved by the differentiation of commodities into commodities and money.

At the same rate, then, as the transformation of the products of labour into commodities is accomplished, one particular commodity is transformed into money.[13]*

It might be argued, however, that Marx's analysis of the commodity rules out a purely formal analysis of the exchange abstraction because, to Marx, the abstractness of value always transmits itself to labour and finds its real meaning in abstract human labour as the economic substance of value. On the other hand, there are places where Marx contemplates the exchange relation between commodities taking a certain shape independently of the quantitative aspect. But even where the form of value is considered as related to labour this relation is often presented as an implication consequent upon the formal characteristics of exchange. Particularly is this the case where the law of value is shown in its actual mode of operation.

Men do not therefore bring the product of their labour into relation with each other as value because they see these objects merely as the material integuments of homogeneous human labour. The reverse is true: by equating their different products to each other in exchange as values, they equate their different kinds of labour as human labour. They do this without being aware of it.[14]

And more clearly:

The production of commodities must be fully developed before the scientific conviction emerges, from experience itself, that all the different kinds of private labour (which are carried on independently of each other, and yet, as spontaneously developed branches of the social division of labour, are in a situation of all-round dependence on each other) are continually being reduced to the quantitative proportions in which society requires them. The reason for this reduction is that in the midst of the accidental and ever-fluctuating

---

* Translation slightly modified by me – S.-R. The creation of coined money first occurring around 680 B.C. on the Ionian side of the Greek Aegean is a safe indication that the conversion of products into commodities and the technical needs of commercial practice had reached an advanced stage. We shall refer to this fact later.

exchange relations between the products, the labour-time socially necessary to produce them asserts itself as a regulative law of nature. In the same way, the law of gravity asserts itself when a person's house collapses on top of him. The determination of the magnitude of value by labour-time is therefore a secret hidden under the apparent movements in the relative values of commodities.[15]

Surely the exchange relations must have the formal ability to weave a web of social coherence among the mass of private individuals all acting independently of one another before, by the action of these exchange relations, their labour spent on all the multi-variety of products can be quantified proportionately to the social needs.

Very probably a case could be made for either interpretation from the text of Marx's writings, but neither shall I employ the length of time required for such a Marxological controversy, nor shall I make my conviction dependent upon its outcome. I shall define the purely formal capacity of the exchange abstraction and its social function as I see it and proceed to prove its reality on the evidence of detailed analysis. This conviction of mine, that the 'commodity form', to use Marx's expression, can be analysed as a phenomenon of its own, in separation from the economic issues, does mark a difference from the Marxian theory but only in the sense that it adds to this theory. The formal analysis of the commodity holds the key not only to the critique of political economy, but also to the historical explanation of the abstract conceptual mode of thinking and of the division of intellectual and manual labour, which came into existence with it. One thing is certain, the rights or wrongs of my deviation from Marx cannot be decided in the abstract, but only in the light of the results.

People become aware of the exchange abstraction only when they come face to face with the result which their own actions have engendered 'behind their backs' as Marx says. In money the exchange abstraction achieves concentrated representation, but a mere functional one – embodied in a coin. It is not recognisable in its true identity as abstract form, but disguised as a thing one carries about in one's pocket, hands out to others, or receives from them. Marx says explicitly that the value abstraction never assumes a representation as such, since the only expression it ever finds is the equation of one commodity with the use-value of another. The gold or silver or other matter which lends to money its palpable and visible body is merely a metaphor of the value abstraction it embodies, not this abstraction itself.

But I set out to argue that the abstractness operating in exchange and reflected in value does nevertheless find an identical expression, namely the abstract intellect, or the so-called 'pure understanding' – the cognitive source of scientific knowledge.

To prove this to be the true historical explanation of the enigmatic 'cognitive faculties' of civilised man we must carry out an isolated analysis of the formal characteristics of commodity exchange in complete methodological separation from any consideration of the magnitude of value and the role of human labour associated with it. These considerations are concerned with the economics of exchange and have been dealt with by Marx in his critique of political economy, and remain unaffected by our enquiry. Equally unaffected are the forms of consciousness which are part of the economic life of society and all those mental forms residing under the name of 'ideologies'. These do not concern our present study, which is to be understood as an attempt purely at a critique of idealistic epistemology, comp-lementary to Marx's critique of political economy, but based on a systematic foundation of its own.

6

The Analysis of the Exchange Abstraction

(a) STATING THE QUESTION

In commodity-producing societies the significance and historical necessity of the exchange abstraction in its spatio-temporal reality is that it provides the form of the social synthesis. None of the activities of production and consumption, on which the life of every individual depends, could take place in the social system of the division of labour without the intervention of commodity exchange. Every economic crisis is an object lesson of the truth that production and consumption are disrupted in proportion to the degree that the exchange nexus fails. Here we shall abstain from entering into any economic aspects of the problem which lie outside the scope of our argument. It is enough to assure ourselves that the synthesis of commodity-producing societies is to be found in commodity exchange, or, more precisely, in the exchange abstraction itself. Thus we must carry out the form analysis of the exchange abstraction in answer to the question: *How is social synthesis possible by means of commodity exchange?*

At first sight the phrasing of the question is one that resembles Kant more clearly than it does Marx. There is, however, a good Marxist reason for this. The implied comparison is not between Kant and Marx but between Kant and Adam Smith – between the disciplines they founded: epistemology and political economy. Adam Smith's *Wealth of Nations* of 1776 and Kant's *Critique of Pure Reason* of 1781 are, above all others, the two works which, in completely unconnected fields and in total systematic independence from each other, strive towards the same goal: to prove the perfect normalcy of bourgeois society.

Assuming that it is in the nature of human labour to produce commodity values, Adam Smith proves that society is best served by allowing unimpeded freedom to every private owner to do as he pleases with his property. Whether for the good of society, as Adam Smith was convinced, or for its undoing, as Ricardo began to suspect, they believed this was in conformity with the norms inherent in human society. We know Marx's commodity analysis served to demolish this very basic assumption on which rests the whole system of political economy, and from his critique Marx uncovers the true inner dialectic of bourgeois society.

Kant's work does not presuppose that it is in the nature of the human mind to perform its labour in separation from manual labour, but it leads to that conclusion. Certainly he seldom mentions manual labour and the 'labouring classes', although he never doubts their social place. But this place in society has no bearing upon the possibility of the workings of the human mind. The theory of 'pure mathematics' and of 'pure science' triumphs in the very fact that it owes no debt to manual labour. Indeed Kant's task was to explain how these two disciplines were possible, on an *a priori* basis in the mind. The empiricist arguments of Hume impeded Kant because they cast doubt upon the apodeictic value of the categories of the pure understanding and only this value could warrant the division of knowledge according to principles *a priori* and principles of *a posteriori*. This meant the singling out of a part of our being which is underivable from our physical and sensorial nature, and which carries the possibilities of pure mathematics and pure science. Thus a bourgeois order of society understood as a division between the educated and labouring classes would form naturally if left to itself, without having to rely on privileges from birth or religion and without curtailing freedom of thought. The fewer obstacles placed in the way of men's public activities the better served will be the common weal by morality, justice and intellectual progress.[16] This, according to Kant, is the only way, founded on reason, by which society can maintain itself in keeping with the conditions of freedom. That this order concealed within itself the class division was a fact hidden to Kant as it was to the other philosophers of the bourgeois enlightenment. Marx called Kant's contribution 'the philosophy of the French Revolution', not least because of this illusion. But the division between the 'educated' and 'labouring' classes was the concept under whose auspices the bourgeois society of economically undeveloped Germany continued to take shape, in contrast to the concepts of capital and labour in the West, where political economy ruled bourgeois thinking. What place here has our own 'critique of epistemology'?

The presuppositions of Kant's epistemology are quite correct in so far as the exact sciences are indeed created by mental labour in total separation from and independence of the manual labour carried on in production. The division between head and hand, and particularly in relation to science and technology, has an importance for bourgeois class rule as vital as that of the private ownership of the means of production. It is only too evident in many of the socialist countries today that one can abolish property rights and still not be rid of class. The class antagonism of capital and labour is linked intrinsically with the division of head and hand. But the connection is hidden to consciousness. In their conceptual terms they are disparate, and it is for that reason that the critique of epistemology must be undertaken independently from that of political economy.

We could phrase our question, omitting the word 'synthesis', by asking: 'How is a social nexus possible by means of commodity exchange?' But the use of the word 'synthesis', in a meaning strange to English readers, allows the convenient adjective 'socially synthetic', which is crucial for our purpose. Moreover the term 'synthetic society' distinguishes the 'man-made' structure of exchange society from primitive tribal society. But I use this term in a different sense and with another range of meaning from that of 'social synthesis'. The first 'synthetic' applies only to commodity societies, the second 'social synthesis' is understood as a general and basic condition of human existence, with no historical limits. In this last sense the word 'synthesis' is used to arm the formulation of my enquiry with a spearhead against Kant's hypostasis of an *a priori* synthesis from the spontaneity of mind, and thus to pay transcendental idealism back in its own coin.

It must be pointed out that none of these meanings of 'synthesis' is absolutely essential to our argument. The deduction of the pure understanding from the exchange abstraction can be presented without anti-idealist thrusts, but the polemical perspective offers the advantage of emphasising the critical character of Marxian thought. The present-day authority-based dogmatisation of Marxism permits it to legitimise an unavowed existence of class division. If its critical force is restored it should help to free Marxism from ossification and renew its creative power.

Some measure of accord underlies our polemical opposition to Kant. We agree that the principles of knowledge fundamental to the quantifying sciences cannot be traced to the physical and sensorial capacity of experience. The exact sciences belong to the resources of an epoch of production which has finally outstripped the limitations of individual pre-capitalist handicrafts. Kant compiles knowledge dualistically from principles *a posteriori* and principles *a priori*. Of these the first correspond to the contribution of the individual senses which never extend beyond the 'receptivity' of our five senses, and the second to the universal scope of concepts linked to mathematics. The scientific experiment strictly corresponds to this dualism of Kant. It is often misinterpreted as an activity of manual labour complementing the intellectual labour of the mathematical hypothesis to be tested. But in fact the experiment is constructed to reduce the individual action to little more than reading the data from scientific instruments. The evidence only has certainty for the individual who reads the data, everyone else must take it on trust. But the concepts based on mathematics are universally valid for the whole of society. The human factor must be eliminated for the sake of scientific objectivity. Logical necessity attaches exclusively to the mathematical hypothesis and the inferences drawn from it. The duality of the sources of knowledge we accept as an incontrovertible fact. The question we ask is, what is the historical origin of our logical ability to construct mathematical hypotheses and the elements contributing to them?

Neither Kant nor any other bourgeois thinker has pursued this enquiry consistently. In the opening sentence of the Introduction to the second edition of the *Critique* the question is intimated but subsequently fades out. Kant gathers the contributory factors into one fundamental principle: the 'originally synthetic unity of the apperception', but for this principle itself he knows no better explanation than to attribute it to a 'transcendental spontaneity' of its own. The explanation turns into the fetishism of what was to be explained. From then on, in the idealist's mind, a time- and space-bound account of the 'capacity of pure understanding' simply cannot exist. The mere suggestion becomes one of the holiest taboos in the tradition of philosophical thought. Nietzsche's scorn over Kant's question 'How are synthetic, *a priori*, judgements possible?' and his answer 'through a capacity' – is totally justified. Nietzsche himself had nothing better to offer. The taboo presupposes that the existing division between head and hand is in its very nature timeless – and this said, bourgeois order must run according to its self-appointed norms until the end of time.

We now confront Kant's question with our own: 'How is social synthesis possible in the forms of commodity exchange?' This question stands outside the entire epistemological sphere of reference. Were it not that we lay some store by a phrasing parallel to Kant's, we could just as well ask: 'Where does the abstractness of money originate?' Both wordings are confined to the time- and space-bound framework of historical-materialist thought and yet both focus on form abstractions which straddle both economics and science. It seems unlikely that we shall fail to find a connection between them if we pursue our question to its roots.

(b) PRACTICAL SOLIPSISM

At first sight it is not obvious how commodity exchange serves as the means of the social synthesis between individuals possessing commodities in private ownership. For commodity exchange is itself a relationship ruled by the principles of private property. Marx writes

> Things are in themselves external to man and therefore alienable. In order that this alienation [*Veraeusserung*] may be reciprocal, it is only necessary for men to agree tacitly to treat each other as the private owners of those alienable things, and, precisely for that reason, as persons who are independent of each other. But this relationship of reciprocal isolation and foreignness does not exist for the members of a primitive community of natural origin. . . .[17]

From this it might appear that the legal concept of private

property took precedence over the actual relations of exchange in contradiction to our historical-materialist mode of thinking. In reality, however, it is just the reverse. The concept of property is itself only a conceptualisation of the factual necessity of keeping use and exchange separated. The need to exempt from use objects entered for exchange is a simple fact of experience; if it is ignored exchange must cease. But because the content of the experience is a negation there arises from it a prohibition of use which extends to everyone involved in the transactions and becomes the norm for all other similar instances. Only by coming into touch with the practice of exchange does the fact of possession assume the meaning of a general law of property. Exchange has this consequence because it is a relationship between human beings. They cannot relate to each other as they do to nature, for instance killing and robbing each other as they do to animals. Instead they must speak to each other, communicate by signs, or in any case recognise each other as human beings. This, too, is still a simple fact but one that gives rise to norms, because it breaks through the basic relation with nature, replacing it with a social relation between groups. The course of this last process has been convincingly reconstructed by George Thomson in the first chapter of his book *The First Philosophers* and the same idea is expressed by Marx – The owners or 'guardians' of the objects for exchange

> must behave in such a way that each does not appropriate the commodity of the other, and alienate his own, except through an act to which both parties consent. The guardians must therefore recognise each other as owners of private property. This juridical relation, whose form is the contract, whether as part of a developed legal system or not, is a relation between two wills which mirror the economic relation. The content of this juridical relation (or relation of two wills) is itself determined by the economic relation.[18]

To put this in other words, the state of reciprocal independence exists on the basis of commodity production. On this basis, all commodities are used, whether for production or consumption, exclusively in the private sphere of the commodity owners. The social synthesis, on the other hand, seen purely formally, is effected only through the exchange of commodities by their owners, in actions separate from their use. Thus the formalism of the exchange abstraction and of the social synthesis which it creates must be found within the confines of the exchange relation.

A transaction of commodity exchange, for example by process of barter, is the exercise by the two exchanging parties of a reciprocal exclusion of ownership concerning two lots of commodities. It is a relationship of appropriation regulated by reciprocity. Every move in the contest, every proposition made by one party and countered by the other, actuates the principle: mine – hence not yours; yours – hence not mine. What is reciprocated is the exclusion of ownership. The agreement upon which the parties settle signifies a delineation of the separate realms of property of each of them at this particular point of contact. Thus there seems to be nothing between the owners but segregation. How, then, does this operate a social synthesis?

The principle, moreover, also taints the relationship of each party to the objects they exchange. For the interest of each is his own interest and not that of the other; similarly the way each one conceives of his interest is his own, the needs, feelings, thoughts that are involved on both sides are polarised on *whose* they are. A piece of bread that another person eats does not feed me. This is the truth that determines the issues at stake in commodity exchange.

Not *what* two people need or feel or think, but *whose* need, feeling or thought will prevail is what shapes the relationship. Thus one can justifiably say that commodity exchange impels solipsism between its participants. Accordingly commodity exchange does not depend on language, on *what* we communicate to each other. Nothing regarding the essence of things need be communicated. Some semantics for 'yes' and 'no', for pointing to this or that, and to indicate quantity, is sufficient to the essentials of a transaction of exchange whether it is carried on between two village gossips or between two strangers who do not speak each other's language. Ethnologists are acquainted with the incidence of 'silent trade'. To put it in the words of Bertrand Russell it is 'that all my data, in so far as they are matters of fact, are private to me . . .'[19]

Thus one can justifiably say that commodity exchange impels

solipsism. The doctrine that between all people, for every one of them, *solus ipse* (I alone) exist is only a philosophical formulation of the principles that in practice regulate exchange. What the commodity owners *do* in an exchange relation is practical solipsism – irrespective of what they think and say about it. This practical solipsism does not need to coincide with self-interest. Someone who takes part in an act of exchange on behalf of another must obey exactly the same principles. If he does not, then the resulting relation is no longer exchange, but one that is qualitatively different, for instance charity . The principles which concern us here belong to the form of interrelation of commodity exchange, not to the psychology of the individuals involved. It is rather this form that moulds the psychological mechanisms of the people whose lives it rules – mechanisms which they then conceive of as inborn, human nature. This makes itself apparent in the way that those in subservience often act to the advantage of those above them. They consider themselves to have acted in self-interest although in fact they have merely obeyed the laws of the exchange nexus.* The practical solipsism of commodity ex-changing owners is nothing but the practice of private property as a basis of social relations. And this is not by people's choice but by the material necessity of the stage of development of their productive forces – the umbilical cord that ties human to natural history.

The principle we call 'practical solipsism' is described above as a reciprocal exclusion of ownership. As the two parties mutually recognise each other as private property owners, each exclusion of property in one direction is answered by an equal one in the other. For what in fact makes them agree to the exchange is that the mutual change of possession which they negotiate leaves their opposing areas of property unimpaired. Commodity exchange can thus be formulated as a social interrelationship between sharply delimited, separate areas of property, or, as Marx puts it, a relation between strangers ('ein Verhältnis wechselseitiger Fremdheit'); it opposes people to each other as strangers. All that matters is that, finally, two lots of commodities actually change

---

* Here is not the place to examine the superstructure of advanced capitalism, but a materialist social psychology of the future would certainly be strengthened by integrating the casual relationship between the abstractions of exchange and thought into the theories of Reich, Fromm, Marcuse, etc.

hands. In exchange the action is social, the mind is private. The outcome is a change in the social status of the commodities as owned property.

In what capacity, then, we ask, do the commodities change hands? In what form, precisely, are commodities exchangeable between separate owners?

(c) THE FORM OF EXCHANGEABILITY OF COMMODITIES

Commodities are exchangeable between their private owners exactly in the capacity in which they are the objects of a mutual exclusion of ownership on the part of their owners. This capacity should plainly be the one that makes it impossible for a commodity to be owned simultaneously by two people in separate ownership. The answer seems too trite to put down on paper: it is that every commodity is one as against the rivalling claims of two owners.

However, we have to be careful how we define this oneness. Is it really the commodity that is one? It cannot be the indivisibility of the commodity as a material body. Goods traded as materials, for instance, are divisible down to any fraction of a quantity. The reason why a given object cannot be separately owned by different people has nothing to do with the nature of the object; it is neither its physical oneness or indivisibility, nor its uniqueness in kind, its irreplaceability. If we probe into the matter with sufficient care it is not difficult to see that it is not the oneness of the *commodities* at all that is important, but the singleness of their *existence* – the fact that the commodity is not, like its use-value, the exclusive private datum of a solipsistic self, but belongs to a single world which is common to all the private selves. Although the perception of a thing is as multiple as the people perceiving it, its existence is one. If the existence of one object were divisible the object could indeed be owned simultaneously by separate owners. Each owner could not only experience the world as his 'private datum' but own it as his exclusive property. Everybody could own the world as Robinson Crusoe does his island. We therefore state: that which constitutes the form of exchangeability of commodities is *the singleness of their existence*.

The question remains: how does this form of exchangeability contribute in effecting the social synthesis through exchange?

The answer is simply that it gives the social synthesis its unity. When trading in commodities has reached the stage where it constitutes the all-decisive *nexus rerum* then the 'duplication of the commodity into commodity and money' (Marx) must already have occurred. But the reverse is possible too – that this duplication very soon leads to commodity exchange becoming a decisive medium of social synthesis (a stage first reached in Ionia in the seventh century B.C.) Money, then, acts as the concrete, material bearer of the form of exchangeability of commodities. That this form can be expressed as the oneness of the commodities' existence explains why there attaches to money an essential, functional unity: there can, at bottom, be only one money in the world.[20]* There can, of course, be different currencies, but so long as these do effective monetary service within their own orbit, they must be interchangeable at definite rates and thus communicate to become one, and only one, universal money system.† Thus all communicating societies of exchange effect a functional unity. This applies even to geographically isolated places where exchange systems, when contact with each other is being made, will sooner or later coalesce to form one extended economic nexus. Needless to say, without this essential oneness of the exchange nexus, the very viability of exchange itself breaks down.

The form of exchangeability applies to commodities regardless of their material description. The abstraction comes about by force of the action of exchange, or, in other words, out of the exchanging agents practising their solipsism against each other.

---

* If two different commodities, such as gold and silver, serve simultaneously as measures of value, all commodities will have two separate price-expressions, the price in gold and the price in silver, which will quietly co-exist as long as the ratio of the value of silver to that of gold remains unchanged, say at 15 to 1. However, every alteration in this ratio disturbs the ratio between the gold-prices and the silver-prices of the commodities, and this proves in fact that a duplication of value contradicts the function of that measure.

† There can be exceptional circumstances making for more than one rate. This was so in the 1930s as a result of foreign-exchange controls and before that in 1923 in the German runaway inflation, when the Mark ceased to do effective monetary service before the introduction of the 'Rentemark'. The devaluation of currency went on at such a pace that large firms even paid wage-bills in company currency of their own issue; for instance, 'in Osram money' if I remember right – in terms of Osram bulbs. Neither these private currencies nor the remaining official one had effective general exchangeability within their own home market and no international rate either. Germany then offered the very rare picture of a modern exchange society without a socially synthetic currency.

The abstraction belongs to the interrelationship of the exchanging agents and not to the agents themselves. For it is not the individuals who cause the social synthesis but their actions. And their actions do it in such a way that, at the moment it happens, the actors know nothing of it.

These are some of the extraordinary paradoxes of a relationship in which men act of their own will, among themselves, with no external interference from nature nor from outside sources. Nothing seems to be beyond their ken; their actions are by mutual agreement for their own benefit, and yet they are enmeshed in the most unsuspected contradictions. We face a pure abstraction but it is a spatio-temporal reality which assumes separate representation in money, a relationship which is formalised only on standards of purely human understanding. Money is an abstract thing, a paradox in itself – a thing that performs its socially synthetic function without any human understanding. And yet no animal can ever grasp the meaning of money; it is accessible only to man. Take your dog with you to the butcher and watch how much he understands of the goings on when you purchase your meat. It is a great deal and even includes a keen sense of property which will make him snap at a stranger's hand daring to come near the meat his master has obtained and which he will be allowed to carry home in his mouth. But when you have to tell him 'Wait, doggy, I haven't paid yet!' his understanding is at an end. The pieces of metal or paper which he watches you hand over, and which carry your scent, he knows, of course; he has seen them before. But their function as money lies outside the animal range. It is not related to our natural or physical being, but comprehensible only in our interrelations as human beings. It has reality in time and space, has the quality of a real occurrence taking place between me and the butcher and requiring a means of payment of material reality. The meaning of this action registers exclusively in our human minds and yet has definite reality outside it – a social reality, though, sharply contrasting with the natural realities accessible to my dog. Here we have the spheres of the 'first' and 'second nature' which we distinguished earlier side by side, and unmistakably divided.

(d) ABSTRACT QUANTITY AND THE POSTULATE OF THE EXCHANGE EQUATION

Penetrating further into the exchange abstraction we notice that there are indeed two abstractions interlocked with each other. The first springs from the separation of exchange from use and has already been discussed. The second operates within the very relationship itself, and results from the interplay of the exchanging parties as solipsistic owners. It attaches directly to the act of exchange itself.

Exchange contains a postulate of the equality of the two lots of commodities to be exchanged. How do we define this equality? The equality is not the identity of the commodities since only *different* commodities are exchanged for one another. Nor are they equal in the evaluation of the exchanging agents, as it would reduce their action to an absurdity if they did not see an advantage to themselves in performing it. Moreover, evaluations are comparable only within one person's consciousness; between persons they are incomparable. But the essence of the postulate of equality in exchange is precisely that it cuts across the gap of experience that separates the exchanging owners. The postulate of equality in exchange does not spring from their experience at all. They merely agree that two lots of commodities are exchangeable. Acting upon this agreement they transfer these commodities from one to the other. One lot moves from *A* to *B*, the other from *B* to *A*, both property transfers being interlinked by each being the condition for the other to take place. The fact that the transfers occur upon this basis equates the two lots of different commodities. They are equated by virtue of being exchanged, they are not exchanged by virtue of any equality which they possess. In this way the relationship between the exchanging persons is transferred to the commodities and expressed as equality between these objects.

It might be said, of course, that given commodities at certain ratios could not be exchanged, unless they were the products of equal amounts of labour. This is a rule dictated by the necessities of the economy within the context of an entire society and its external trade relations. Viewed from this economic aspect it is true to say that commodities exchange in accordance with the amount of labour stored up in them. Our analysis, however, is not concerned with the economics of exchange, but solely with exchange as a peculiar form of social interrelationship between individuals. 'Their quantitative exchange relation is at first determined purely by chance'.[21] There is nothing in the formal constitution of exchange that could predetermine its quantitative relationship. A man dying of thirst in the desert would 'exchange' his worldly possessions for a drink of water.

Let us be quite explicit then, that the transference of human relations to relations between things, in other words, the 'reifying' (*verdinglichende*) property of exchange is bound up with the equating effect which the act of exchange exercises upon the objects. The underlying reason for this alienating effect of exchange is that, on the basis of commodity production, it is property, not the labour of production, which governs the social order by operating the social synthesis.

The act of exchange postulating the equality of the commodities could be preceded by a barter in which each of the commodity owners haggles for 'more to take' and 'less to give'. True, commodities are traded in lots measured in dimensional quantities of tons or gallons or acres, etc. But the comparatives of 'more' and 'less' used in a deal of exchange do not imply a quantitative comparison between, say, tons of coal and reams of paper, or of acres of land and yards of linen. The interrelational equation posited by an act of exchange leaves all dimensional measurements behind and establishes a sphere of non-dimensional quantity. This is the pure or abstract quality of cardinal numbers, with nothing to define it but the relation of greater than ($>$) or smaller than ($<$) or equal to ($=$) some other quantity as such. In other words, the postulate of the exchange equation abstracts quantity in a manner which constitutes the foundation of free mathematical reasoning.

According to this argument mathematical reasoning should be found to emerge at the historical stage at which commodity exchange becomes the agent of social synthesis, a point in time marked by the introduction and circulation of coined money. And it is interesting to note that Pythagoras, who first used mathematical thought in its deductive character, followed after the first spread of coinage in the seventh and sixth centuries B.C. and is now believed to have himself been instrumental in instituting a system of coinage in Kroton, where he emigrated from Samos around 540 B.C.

But the discussion of how the form-elements of the exchange abstraction are reflected in consciousness must be postponed as we are still engaged with the analysis of the real abstraction itself.

(e) ABSTRACT TIME AND SPACE

The abstraction of pure quantity gains in importance by its association with a corresponding abstraction occurring to time and space when they apply to acts of exchange instead of to acts of use. In use, understood as the entire sphere of man's inter-exchange with nature, time and space are inseparaby linked with the events of nature and the material activities of man, with the ripening of the crops, the sequence of the seasons, the hunting of animals, with man's birth and death and all that happens in his life-span. The business of exchange enforces abstraction from all this, for the objects of exchange are assumed to remain immutable for the duration of the transaction. This transaction takes its time, including that of the delivery of the commodities and the act of payment upon the conclusion of the deal. But this time is emptied of the material realities that form its contents in the sphere of use. The same applies to space, say to the distance which the commodities have to travel when changing owners. Exchange empties time and space of their material contents and gives them contents of purely human significance connected with the social status of people and things. These are contents of man's own making over which he ought to exercise unimpeded control.

While commodities travel a distance for delivery to their new owners, the equation between the two lots prevails at every one spot and every one moment the same as at every other one. Time and space when applying to exchange are thus supposed to be absolutely homogeneous. They are also continuous in the sense that they allow for registering any interruption occurring in the progress of the commodities in order not to upset their exchange equation.

Time and space rendered abstract under the impact of commodity exchange are marked by homogeneity, continuity and emptiness of all natural and material content, visible or invisible (e.g. air). The exchange abstraction excludes everything that makes up history, human and even natural history. The entire empirical reality of facts, events and description by which one moment and locality of time and space is distinguishable from another is wiped out. Time and space assume thereby that character of absolute historical timelessness and universality which must mark the exchange abstraction as a whole and each of its features.

(*f*) THE CONCEPT OF VALUE

The contradiction between the postulated equality and the empirical difference of the commodities is such that it could not be handled without the invention of the term 'value' so that the equality can be denoted as 'equivalence' related to exchange. But value does not create the equality, it only applies to it *post festum*. The term by itself, as value in exchange, has no thought content of its own, no definable logical substance. It simply articulates contradictory social relations uniformly by quantitative differentiation of things according to the facts of exchange.

Marx repeatedly emphasises that the concept of value bears no inherent reference to labour. The reference of value to labour, or rather the determination of value by labour, is not a conscious one, but takes place blindly, by the functional effect of the social exchange process as a whole:

> by equating their different products to each other as values, they equate their different kinds of labour as human labour. They do this without being aware of it. Value, therefore, does not have its description branded on its forehead; it rather transforms every product of labour into a social hieroglyphic.[22]

And in a footnote he adds:

> When, therefore, Galiani says: 'Value is a relation between persons, . . . he ought to have added: a relation concealed beneath a material shell.' The determination of the magnitude of value by labour-time is . . . a secret hidden under the apparent movements of the relative values of the commodities. Its discovery destroys the semblance of the merely accidental

determination of the magnitude of the value of the products of labour, but by no means abolishes that determination's material form.[23]

In a famous letter addressed to Kugelmann on 11 July 1868 the rationale of this social mechanism is expressed in very simple terms. Any human society, regardless of its formation and material stage of development, is viable only if it succeeds in directing the available social labour force in the right proportion to serve the existing social needs. In a society based on what Marx calls a communal mode of production where work is carried out in a directly social way, i.e. collectively, or if done separately, in a manner permitting every worker to know what every other one is doing, this socially indispensable direction of social labour is done by the labourers themselves, or on their behalf by agreement and by planning. But commodity production arises when, because of the development of the productive forces, these communal ties break up and the producers work as private producers acting independently of each other. Then the social network depends on the activities, not of the producers, but of the owners, activated by the interest in their property. This activity takes on, in one way or another, the form of exchange. 'And in a society where the network of social labour establishes itself through the private exchange of the individual products of labour, the form in which this proportional distribution of labour ensues is precisely the exchange value of the products.'[24]

Hence any society based on private production must be governed by the laws of exchange in order to survive. This holds true regardless of the stage of commodity production.

These indispensable laws of exchange, which hold out a promise of parity under the postulate of equivalence, do not lose their grip on society when they turn into their opposite, namely into laws of the imparity of surplus-value for capital out of labour. The laws of exchange apply to the labourer forced to sell his labour-power as commodity to a capitalist wanting to use that commodity to his own advantage under the same formal principle as they do to the selling and buying of any other commodity. However, measured by the economic realities of the case, the principle of equivalence proves to be nothing more than form – a form in contradiction to its content and therefore amounting to a sham and yet remaining no less indispensable for that reason.

> The relation of exchange subsisting between capitalist and labourer becomes a mere semblance belonging only to the process of circulation, it becomes a mere form which is alien to the content of the transaction and merely mystifies it [. . . and yet] however much the capitalist mode of appropriation may seem to fly in the face of the original laws of commodity production, it nevertheless arises, not from violation, but, on the contrary, from the application of these laws. [25]

In fact so little does the capitalist exploitation of labour constitute a breach of the formal principles of exchange that it is only 'from the moment there is a free sale, by the worker himself, of labour power as a commodity . . . that commodity production is generalised and becomes the typical form of production; it is only from then onwards that, from the first, every product is produced for sale and all wealth produced goes through the sphere of circulation. Only where wage-labour is its basis does commodity production impose itself upon society as a whole; but it is also true that only there does it unfold all its hidden potentialities.'[26] Marx does not specify what 'potentialities' he had in mind when he wrote this. But the developments of science and technology might well have been part of them.

One must realise the importance of the distinction which Marx draws in his analysis of the commodity between the 'form of value' (or 'form of commodity') and the 'magnitude of value'. The changing form of labour, as slave-labour, serf-labour, wage-labour, and the corresponding differences in the determination of the magnitude of value are decisive for the system of economy prevailing in the different stages of development of commodity production. The unvarying formal features of exchange, on the contrary, constitute a mechanism of real abstraction indispensable for the social synthesis throughout and supplying a matrix for the abstract conceptual reasoning characteristic of all societies based on commodity production. While in history the economy on the one hand, and the forms and tasks of reasoning on the other, interact in intricate ways, it is profitable for historical materialism to analyse both aspects of commodity exchange in detail. Marx's analysis shows that it is impossible to understand the economics of commodity production without a great deal of attention to its formal characteristics and contradictions, and Marx never tires of stressing their importance and of blaming the bourgeois mentality for its imperviousness to them.

The formal features of commodity exchange and of value play a part which not only permit but demand separate analysis. And the need for such an analysis lies in the exposure of the fetish character of intellectual labour in its division from manual labour.

(g) SUBSTANCE AND ACCIDENTS

It has been shown that the forms of the exchange abstraction are parts of the act of exchange; they constitute the laws by which exchange operates. The commodities must not be exposed to physical change. Their condition is thus materially constant, and although this is merely a postulate, it is a socially necessary one. That means that on the standard of the act of exchange, the commodities are positively qualityless. On the other hand, as they are only exchanged for the purpose of use they present themselves to the exchanging agents in the garb of their use-values. Thus they exist in a twofold capacity on the market; in that of the qualityless condition and in the qualitative splendour of their use-value. The property of qualitylessness is what gives them their reality in exchange, while their use-properties are only stored in the minds of people.

In the course of the evolution of exchange the necessities of trade enforce 'the differentiation of commodities into commodities and money'. As a result the intrinsic duality of the commodity as such takes on the shape of an external contrast. The qualityless abstractness of the object of exchange is semi-concealed in the uniformity of money. As non-descriptive matter does not exist in nature, gold, silver, copper, etc., or simply paper must stand in for it. These empirical materials serve their abstract function, however, in a purely metaphorical capacity and cannot, therefore, impair the duality at its root.

Later on we shall recognise in this duality the well-known relationship of substance and accidents. These are conceptual terms, whereas our analysis here is still concerned with the exchange abstraction in its real state only.

(h) ATOMICITY

In order that this non-descriptive substance can stand as equivalent for every exchangeable commodity and in any proportion of it the material of money must, in apparent contradiction to its qualityless integrity, be adaptable according to every possible quantity of value. It must therefore be divisible *ad lib.* Money must be divisible in order to leave the commodities undivided. This is one of the contradictions with which the social function of money confronts the mind through the mediation of its form. The abstract materiality of value or of the subject of the exchange-equation figures as an integral whole in every single incident of exchange, and in order to be able to serve all incidents in this capacity it must, on the contrary, allow for any degree of divisibility, or as the corresponding philosophical term has it, for sheer atomicity.

'As a value, every commodity is equally divisible; in its natural existence this is not the case.'[27] What brings the unlimited divisibility of matter into play is 'value' and the exchange abstraction underlying it; it is not the natural existence of things material.

(i) ABSTRACT MOVEMENT

How do we have to describe the actual transfer of the commodities which their owners have agreed to exchange? We know that it is a physical act which must leave the physical state of the commodities unchanged. True, this is no more than a postulate, but without it exchange would be rendered impossible. It must therefore serve as the standard for the description of the act by which the exchange agreement concluded between the owners of the commodities is carried out. Accordingly the act of exchange has to be described as *abstract movement through abstract (homogeneous, continuous, and empty) space and time of abstract substances (materially real but bare of sense-qualities) which thereby suffer no material change and which allow for none but quantitative differentiation (differentiation in abstract, non-dimensional quantity).* Being the aim of the whole relationship and of the separation of exchange from use, this description of the movement of the commodities in their circulation comprises the exchange abstraction in all its elements. It also shares the same conversion of the actual historical happening into historical timelessness and universality which attaches to the abstractness of time and space as dimensions of commodity exchange.

The movement of the commodities can vary, it can suffer interruptions or take devious ways, while time and space maintain their abstract uniformity. But whatever the vicissitudes of their movement through the processes of circulation may be, the commodities are supposed to retain throughout the value at which they were bought. While this constancy of their exchange-value conveys an overall continuity to the act of transfer, the movement can at any place and time be stopped and the state and value of the commodities be reascertained, and this provision cuts their movement into discrete moments. Both continuity and discreteness attach to the abstract movement of the commodities side by side. This contradictory nature accrues to the movement of the commodities from the social origin of its abstractness. In antiquity it has given rise to the paradoxes of Zeno, whereas in modern times it has been absorbed in the analysis of movement by means of the calculus.

(j) STRICT CAUSALITY

The exchange abstraction is not the source of the concept of causality – that goes back much further. It does, however, seem to be the root of the cause and effect equation which characterises strict causality. As we see it, strict causality is the form in which physical change affects objects which are up for exchange on the market under the postulate exempting them from material change. Changes caused by human beings which infringe this postulate are outlawed by the police authority presiding in the market. The concept of exemption from material change is in effect nothing more than a fiction whereby the reality of material change is not excluded but is subjected to a specific conceptual form. This is the form of the exact, mathematically formulatable equation between cause and effect by which the process of causality, if it can be isolated as a specific single event, submits, before and after its completion, to the postulate negating material change. The negation of change would accordingly be the logical postulate from which the strict equation between cause and effect derives its necessity as thought.

Here there becomes visible the root of a new concept of nature and of natural change sharply distinct from any magical and mythological modes of thinking. It is the concept of processes which occur not only purely naturally, without any human interference, but which gain ground in the market despite all measures to the contrary and despite the social postulate exempting commodities from all material change. In such processes nature operates as a force transcending all collusion with man, a force totally separated from the human sphere; nature is, in other words, nothing more than pure object world. The concept of pure causality is thus related to this as a process of cause and effect occurring solely within the object world.

This conception of nature is unmistakably at odds with the nature experienced by man in the labour process of which Marx says that man, when he acts upon nature, is a force of nature himself. As an agent of the market, man is hardly less divided from nature than the value of the commodities themselves.

The concept of causality and its strict form expression contain, of course, just like any other 'category of pure reason', not the slightest trace of any such social origin; indeed any thought of such an origin appears as a complete impossibility. But this is in no way an objection to the present analysis. It will be shown that this genetic blindness of the categories of understanding finds its fitting explanation in the reflection of the exchange abstraction, for the content of this abstraction has in all its features a strictly timeless form which is irreconcilable with any thought of a specific origin. From being historical and geographical in character these features become subject solely to mathematical determination.

Causality, or, more exactly, its form determination as strict causality, constitutes an exception among the categories examined here. It is not part of the exchange abstraction, but a consequence, a corollary of it. The action of exchange permits of no material change to the objects whether the cause of this change be considered adequate or not. Thus strict causality, so far as I can see, performs no socially synthetic function. It has been included in the analysis only so as to forestall criticism of its omission among the 'categories of pure reason'. And indeed the principle of causality is never directly employed in mathematical science; it occurs only as a means of experimentally verifying hypotheses of motion. It is the pure scheme of motion that is the actually operative form abstraction generated by the abstraction of exchange.

(k) CONCLUDING REMARKS TO THE ANALYSIS

The pattern of movement inherent in the exchange abstraction introduces then a definitive concept of nature as material object world, a world from which man, as the subject of social activities, has withdrawn himself. We said that, in terms of the exchange abstraction, time becomes unhistorical time and space ungeographical space; indeed they become abstract time and abstract space, endless time and limitless space. In terms of this form determination time and space provide the setting for a conception of nature which is in antithetic contrast to society. This idea of nature is novel to eras of commodity production and incompatible with any of the anthropomorphisms of tribal societies based on communal modes of production.

We noticed that the exchange pattern of abstract movement has a peculiar contradiction at its root. In exchange, abstraction must be made from the physical nature of the commodities and from any changes that could occur to it. No events causing material changes to the commodities are admissible while the exchange transaction is in progress. On the other hand, the act of property transfer involved in the transaction is a physical act itself, consisting of real movements of material substances through time and space. Hence the exchange process presents a physicality of its own, so to speak, endowed with a status of reality which is on a par with the material physicality of the commodities which it excludes. Thus the negation of the natural and material physicality constitutes the positive reality of the abstract social physicality of the exchange processes from which the network of society is woven.

What I distinguish here as two contrasting 'physicalities' – the one, concrete and material, comprising commodities as objects of use and our own activities as material, inter-exchange with nature; the other, abstract and purely social, concerning commodities as objects of exchange and quantities of value – these two can, as we have said in German, be termed 'erste Natur' (primary or elementary nature) and 'zweite Natur' (second and purely social man-made or synthetic nature). Both are real in time and space; primary nature is created by human labour, second nature is ruled by relations of property.

We must now establish the great importance of the following, initially elusive fact: by its own physicality in terms of spatio-temporal action the abstraction from natural physicality, which exchange enforces by its separation from use, establishes itself as a physicality in the abstract or as a kind of *abstract nature*. It is devoid of all sense reality and admits only of quantitative differentiation. Furthermore it is understandable solely to people acquainted with money and engaged in the use and acquisition of it – that is, only to members of that thoroughly synthetic society which Friedrich Engels classes as 'civilisation' and which first begins with classical Greek antiquity.[28] This abstract and purely social physicality of exchange has no existence other than in the human mind, but it does not spring from the mind. It springs from the activity of exchange and from the necessity for it which arises owing to the disruption of communal production into private production carried on by separate individuals independently of each other.

This real abstraction is the arsenal from which intellectual labour throughout the eras of commodity exchange draws its conceptual resources. It was the historical matrix of Greek philosophy and it is still the matrix of the conceptual paradigms* of science as we know it. Basic changes occurring in these paradigms indicate major changes of this matrix, and vice versa, because the socially necessary forms of cognition in any epoch have no source from which they can originate other than the prevailing functionalism of the social synthesis. Up to the nineteenth century this functionalism has undergone important modifications, but only in the twentieth century and from the beginning of monopoly capitalism has it suffered structural changes.

---

* I use this term in the sense of Thomas S. Kuhn's *The Structure of Scientific Revolution* (Chicago: Univ. of Chicago Press, 1962). Kuhn has successfully distinguished different paradigms. I believe that it is also possible to explain them.

7

The Evolution of Coined Money

The analysis in the foregoing chapters concerns a formal aspect of commodity exchange which might seem to be common to exchange of all ages, so that the question occurs as to why commodity exchange gives rise to abstract thinking only at the relatively late date of classical antiquity and not from the very first exchange, probably tens of thousands of years earlier. We have seen from our analysis that commodity exchange serves as a means of social synthesis only from Greek antiquity onwards, but we now ask what distinguishes it then from previous stages. We must therefore very briefly peruse the main phases of development of exchange with an eye to their formal characteristics.

In a mere isolated, accidental case of exchange between any two parties the exchange abstraction evidently shows no trace at all. At a higher stage, which Marx calls 'the expanded form of value', when exchange becomes multilateral and comprises a variety of commodities, one of these must serve as a means of exchange of the others. Here too, this role does not convey to the commodity in question any appearance different from its use-value, although the latter is now vested with a postulate not to undergo any material change while it acts in this capacity. Still, the choice for this role falls upon a commodity which by its physical durability, divisibility and mobility easily complies with the postulate. In this way the postulate of immutability, although springing from the nature of exchange, soon again appears to all concerned to be the outcome of the peculiar use-value of the commodity in question. The fact that a peculiar halo is likely to accrue to the latter will seem to confirm rather than to contradict the misleading appearance. This is notoriously so when the role of equivalent settles upon one or the other of the precious metals. 'All this was still very undeveloped; the precious metals were beginning to be the predominant and general money commodity, but still uncoined, exchanging simply by their naked weight',[29] that is, in the appearance of objects of use.

Therefore at each transaction they had to be weighed and cut or melted and tested for their metallic purity; in short, they had to be treated in accordance with their physical nature. But precisely this was the reason why they did not conform very well to the requirements of the market, and their inadequacies were not remedied until the invention of coinage. This portentous step was taken for the first time in history about 680 B.C. on the Ionian side of the Aegean, in Lydia or Phrygia. The institution quickly spread, following, as well as helping, the marked commercial expansion in process at that epoch and finding imitation in the main Greek centres of maritime trade. The very introduction of coinage is a sure sign of commodity production entering upon its stage of 'full growth'.

In coinage the previous relationship by which the value status of a commodity serving as money was subordinated to, and covered up by, its material status is reversed. A coin has it stamped upon its body that it is to serve as a means of exchange and not as an object of use. Its weight and metallic purity are guaranteed by the issuing authority so that, if by the wear and tear of circulation it has lost in weight, full replacement is provided. Its physical matter has visibly become a mere carrier of its social function. A coin, therefore, is a thing which conforms to the postulates of the exchange abstraction and is supposed, among other things, to consist of an immutable substance, a substance over which time has no power, and which stands in antithetic contrast to any matter found in nature.

Anybody who carries coins in his pocket and understands their functions bears in his mind, whether or not he is aware of it, ideas which, no matter how hazily, reflect the postulates of the exchange abstraction. To go about his marketing activities of buying and selling and to take advantage of the power of his money no clearer awareness is required. But to reflect upon the ideas involved, to become conscious of them, to formulate them, to take stock of them and to work out their interrelations, to probe into their uses and their implications, to recognise their antithetic contrast to the world of the senses and yet their intrinsic reference to it, etc. – this does not follow automatically from the use of coined money, it constitutes a clearly definable conditioned potentiality inherent in a monetary economy.

The social upheavals and class struggles ensuing from the development of this economy in the various city-states of ancient Greece created under the existing historical conditions the necessary incentives for tackling these tasks. To work out their solutions occupied the long line of philosophers from Thales to Aristotle throughout three hundred years of astounding intellectual effort. What came into existence here is the capacity of conceptual reasoning in terms of abstract universals, a capacity which established full intellectual independence from manual labour.

8

Conversion of the Real Abstraction into the Conceptual Abstraction

The formal structure of commodity exchange constitutes the core of the second nature: the purely social, abstract, functional reality which I earlier contrasted with primary nature where man exists on the same level as animals. Second nature finds its external expression in money, and in it the specifically human element in us finds its first separate and objectively real manifestation in history. This occurs through the necessity for a social synthesis which is in total separation from any of the operations of man's material interchange with nature. These operations are in themselves part of primary nature, but on the basis of commodity production they are consigned to the private spheres of the commodity owners, irrespective of whether they are operations of production, consumption or reproduction. These countless private spheres must inter-communicate because of the division of labour between them, and they do so by way of commodity exchange.

As I have already pointed out, it is solely the *action* of exchange which exercises its social effect; the consciousness of those involved in it is private and blind to the socially synthetic character of their actions. The consciousness is fully occupied with things from which the action abstracts and only through the unremitting abstractness of the acts of exchange from all things empirical does the nexus of this unconscious society impose itself as one of second nature. Only when labour is translated into the formal terms of second nature, as abstract human labour, does it enter into the nexus under the term of 'value', as value-in-exchange; labour as the substance of value, because second nature is of human origin, cut off from and contrasting to primary nature. Second nature forms the basis of human self-awareness linked to self-alienation, since it operates entirely in the forms of the private appropriation of labour products and in separation from the labour which produces them. For even if the producers themselves exchange their own products they do so, not as producers, but as commodity owners.

Two aspects are thus combined under the single heading 'second nature': its socially synthetic reality in historical time and space and the ideal form of cognition through abstract concepts. The first aspect is crucial for our social existence under conditions of commodity production, the second is fundamental for our scientific knowledge through intellectual labour. By their significance both aspects of the abstraction are so disparate that to view them as two aspects of the same abstraction seems an inacceptable suggestion. And yet, if our understanding of the second nature is correct, this suggestion is inescapable. The abstraction comprising both aspects is one and can only be one. Its two aspects or parts can be related in no other way than in a context of conversion, the real abstraction being converted to its ideal reflection into intellectual form. But not everybody may feel convinced of the identity of the abstraction in its real and its ideal shape and be prepared to accept the fact of the conversion, or rather the ascertainment of it as a foregone conclusion. An effort should therefore be made to demonstrate the conversion.

This is, however, no easy task. How can we set out to reason the case for or against the conversion? Thinking of the conversion as a performance in people's minds, it can, of course, never be either demonstrated or denied because it cannot be witnessed. The concepts in question being non-empirical, their mental presence cannot be testified by observable objects or facts. To try to ask the people themselves is equally non-availing since we have ourselves made out that the conversion must be blotted out from the minds engaged in it. All we can argue is the problem at issue in the conversion and how to make it recognisable. In real life, the ideal abstraction blots out the real abstraction so as to make it irrecognisable. In order to avoid this happening the conversion must be presented as occurring from an act of commodity exchange as its starting-point or in direct context with the handling of coined money for its commercial use. In other words the conversion must be presented as occurring in a way in which it is absolutely impossible for it to occur. That is to say, the reader must understand our presentation to be nothing more than a simulation of an occurrence of the conversion and must be prepared to enter into it as an exercise staged for the sole purpose of demonstrating the cardinal point at issue. We are not concerned here with the history of the conversion and with the rise of the conceptual mode of thinking in ancient Greece and with its developments further on. This will occupy us in the second part of this study. But it would be impossible to appreciate the historical genesis of the intellect and of the division of intellectual from manual labour without first having clarified the nature of the conversion from within.

As it would obviously be impracticable to extend our exercise to cover the entirety of the exchange abstraction, we must select one out of its elements, preferably one that lends itself easily to our purpose. Let us take the question of the material of the coins which a money-owner carries in his pockets on the way to the market. We have said that such a person must carry ideas in his mind which 'reflect the postulates of the exchange abstraction' whether he be conscious of this or not, and we pointed to the material that his coins are made of as an example. How should one describe this material? It may consist of one of the shiny stainless metals normally used for coinage – and our money-owner might, if he behaved like every other one, identify it with one of these, until he becomes aware that it could as well be any of the others – gold, silver, bronze, nickel or what have you. And if he accepted a promissory note it could even be paper. But we have already seen that none of these choices which nature has to offer or which man can make is really true to the description of the material of which money should be made. Why else should the bank issuing money pledge itself to make up for wear and tear? All existing materials, all things and creatures of this world are perishable, transient, deceptive in appearance, corruptible, subject to the effects of time and any other of the deprecatory qualifications which Plato, for one, arrays against them before he speaks of the unblemished, everlasting, self-identical and pure entities which he honours with the title 'ideas'. But are, then, the coins in the pocket of our money-owner mere 'ideas'? At this frightening thought he grabs all the coins he can find in his pocket and ponders. 'These *are* things', he utters, 'and they are things not only for me but for anyone to whom I offer them in payment for the commodities he has to sell. And they have the same reality for every member of this Athenian polis of mine; this universal social reality is in the nature of money, whatever Antiphon or any other Sophist may say about reality attaching only to my perceptions and not to things beyond them. My coins are as real as my body and as the meat they buy for me to feed on, as real therefore as the body of everyone else. Immaterial money, "ideal money", thought-coins – what absurdity! No coin could be money without being materially real'.

Thus he reaches the reassuring conclusion that the material of which his money is made *is* real stuff, as real as any other stuff existing in time and space. And yet, at the same time it is totally different. For it is unchangeable under the effects of time as not only Plato might glory about but the very treasury of our State tells us when issuing our drachma. But how can matter not subjected to time be existing in time? Not in the whole of nature and not in the bounds of sense-perception can such matter be found. How does our money-owner in his exceptional zeal know about it if this matter cannot be seen or felt and even touched? He knows it by thought and nothing else but thought. Never in his life has thought of this obstinate kind come his way, thought of something real and yet detached from all and every sense-quality by which reality is real to us. Being freed from sense-quality his coin-material is indestructible. 'How is it different then', he argues, 'from the reality that Plato terms "ideas"? But brother Plato is wrong in pushing this reality out of our commercial world and gazing at it in the skies only because of its indestructibility. On the contrary, this stable, unchanging, abstractly uniform material of which my coins are made is right here in my pocket.' So he looks at it again and what he holds in his hand is a piece of silver, silver from the mines of Laurion and none of that Platonic stuff which has room for existence only in his pure, abstract thought and for which he knows no definition and no name.

After having got stuck like Socrates on the way to his symposium he now hurries with renewed intent to the agora, the market-place, where he planned his purchases. Arriving there at last he is, however, struck again, for not far from the butcher's stand he sees Plato sitting on the parapet in person in philosophical converse with Socrates, Glaucon, Adeimantus and other friends. Should he accept his coins as being simple silver, go to the butcher and buy his meat with them, or should he pursue the question of the indestructible, abstract and purely ideal stuff he knows his coins should really be made of, and ask Plato to put him wise on the question? This, of course, would engage him in purely intellectual pursuits and who knows when he would ever return to the economic necessities of life?

Well, we can leave our experimental money-owner at the parting of the ways whose incompatible alternative would make him split in two. But he served to demonstrate by his simulations that the alternative itself is no invention but a true duality inherent in the nature of commodity exchange and growing out of the real abstraction when it becomes discernible through its reification in coinage. So long as we move in the sphere of commodity exchange and on the level of market activities coins are pieces of metal. This metal is an object of use-value estranged from its use by serving as the generally recognised equivalent of all other commodities and in its value representing quantitative parcels of social labour in the abstract. But underlying this monetary service of the coins is the general 'commodity abstraction', as Marx calls it, which allows for, and indeed enforces the formation of non-empirical concepts of pure thought when this abstraction becomes mentally identified in its given spatio-temporal reality. But this is an activity absolutely at variance with the basic economic use of the coinage and its links are irrecognisable. We shall return to this in the next chapter; at present we confine ourselves to one aspect of the problem only, the question of identifying the material from which coins should be made.

The first 'pure thinker' emerging with a concept fitting the description of the abstract material of money, but without any idea of what his concept stood for and what had prompted him to conceive it, was the ancient-Greek Parmenides. His $τὸ ἔον$ translated means 'the One; that which is'. It is unchanging through time, fills all space, lacks all properties of sense-perception, is strictly homogeneous and uniform, indivisible, incapable of becoming or of perishing and is for ever at rest (i.e. conforms to the static inertia common to thinking throughout classical antiquity). Parmenides stresses that its reality or being is of such a kind that it is inherently impossible to think that it is not. This piece of reasoning takes pride of place in his teaching and marks the first historical instance of a conclusion based on an argument of logic. It prompted Hegel to say: 'Parmenides marks the beginning of philosophy.'[30] And Francis Cornford agrees: 'He is the first philosopher to argue, formally deducing conclusions from premises, instead of making dogmatic announcements. His school were the originators of dialectic.'[31] Together with Pythagoras and Heraclitus, Parmenides belongs to the first philosophers with whom man's mental activity assumes a shape totally different from the anthropomorphisms associated with the communal modes of production preceding the age of commodity production. With these philosophers, and the great Ionians of the Milesian school before them, we witness the 'Greek miracle': the beginning of the conceptual mode of thinking which is ours to this day and which carries the division of intellectual from manual labour that permeates all class societies based upon commodity production.

It needs to be stressed that neither Parmenides nor any other founder of classical Greek philosophy ever claims to have formed his concepts himself, for example by abstracting from the particular and manifold of a perception to the level of a universal concept. None of them legitimates his concepts by presenting the way they were made. The abstractions underlying them are of a completely different kind; they are found given, ready-made, totally without derivation. They have occurred elsewhere; not by way of human thinking. Thus Parmenides, for example, describes in the allegorical proemium by which he prefaces his philosophy how he has flown up to the dwelling of Dike, the goddess of knowing right and wrong, and there was initiated by her to the wisdom he proclaims. And he adds explicitly that she admonished him: 'Only by means of reason must you ponder the much considered teaching that I give you.'*[32]

Thus without the concept τὸ ἐόν being itself a creation of Parmenides' thinking, it is nevertheless the starting-point for a thinking based on arguments of reason. Central to this is that conceptual thought grasps the dialectic of truth and untruth according to standards of a binding, logical necessity of thought or of contrariety to it. Parmenides argues: 'Thinking and the thought that "it is" are one and the same. For you will not find thought apart from that which is, in respect of which thought is uttered. For there is and shall be no other thing besides what is.' 'That is the fundamental idea', adds Hegel. And indeed Hegel recognises in Parmenides his own conceptual ontologism.[33]

What defines the character of intellectual labour in its full-fledged division from all manual labour is the use of non-empirical form-abstractions which may be represented by nothing other than non-empirical, 'pure' concepts. The explanation of intellectual labour and of this division thus depends on proving the origin of the underlying, non-empirical form-abstractions. This is the task we have undertaken. And we can see that this origin can be none other than the real abstraction of commodity exchange, for it is of a non-empirical form-character and does not spring from thought. This is the only way in which justice can be done to the nature of intellectual labour and of science and yet avoid idealism. It is Greek philosophy which constitutes the first historical manifestations of the separation of head and hand in this particular mode. For the non-empirical real abstraction is

---

*   Here I follow Hegel's rendering in his lectures, op. cit. 387: 'Nur mit der Vernunft must du die vielgeprüfte Lehre erwägen, die ich dir sagen werde.' Hermann Diels translates: 'Mit dem Verstande bringe die vielumstrittene Prufüng, die ich dir riet, zur Entscheidung.' *Fragmente der Vorsokratiker* (1903) p. 119.)

evident in commodity exchange only because through it a social synthesis becomes possible which is in strict spatio-temporal separation from all acts of man's material interchange with nature. And to my knowledge this kind of social synthesis does not reach fruition before the eighth or seventh centuries B.C. in Greece, where the first introduction of coinage around 680 B.C. was of fundamental importance. Thus we are here confronted with the historical origin of conceptual thought in its fully developed form constituting the 'pure intellect' in its separation from all man's physical capacities.

9

The Independent Intellect

(a) SELF-ALIENATION AND SELF-DIRECTION

We have not yet pursued to its conclusion the process of identification which we have chosen as the most exacting means for illustrating the theoretical issue contained in the conversion of the real abstraction of exchange into the ideal abstraction of conceptual thought. This results in the independent intellect.

Only at the final conclusion of the identification are the resulting concepts cut off from their origin; only at this point can it be said that, as abstract thought is engendered, it is cut off from its root, by its root and at its root. This is because the real abstraction of exchange has as its distinguishing mark the total exclusion of empirical content. Its abstractness is non-empirical. Thus, if it or any of its elements are correctly identified, this results in the formation of concepts as non-empirical as the exchange abstraction itself. And being non-empirical, they bear no trace of the locality, the date or any other circumstances of their origin. They stand outside the realm of sense-perception without, however, forfeiting their own prime claim to reality. But this reality is that of being as a whole, not that of any specific object.

It must further be understood that because it is cut off from its social origin, the abstract intellect emerges with a peculiar normative sense all its own, serving as its 'logic'. We have observed this phenomenon when discussing the Parmenidean concept τὸ ἔον especially in the light of Hegel's interpretation. Here the non-empirical conceptual abstraction, when it emerges clearly, proves to be connected from the very beginning with its own sense of truth and untruth and a kind of reasoning characterised by argument of logic. These are the properties which the Greeks understood as the powers of dialectic. Thus the conversion involves both self-alienation and self-direction.

The explanation of this normative sense which carries the logical independence of the abstract intellect and is responsible for its cognitive faculty lies in the very nature of the exchange abstraction. The entire exchange abstraction is founded upon social postulate and not upon fact. It is a postulate that the use of commodities must remain suspended until the exchange has taken place; it is a postulate that no physical change should occur in the commodities and this still applies even if the facts belie it; it is a postulate that the commodities in the exchange relation should count as equal despite their factual difference; it is a postulate that the alienation and acquisition of things between commodity-owners is tied to the condition of exchangeability; it is a postulate that commodities change owners by a translation from one locality to another without being materially affected. None of these form-concepts imply statements of fact. They are all norms which commodity exchange has to obey to be possible and to enable anarchical society to survive by the rules of reification.

(*b*) THE RELATIONAL SHIFT

This statement does not in itself provide the full explanation required. For these postulates apply directly only to social relations and to people's manner of action and are a far cry from the normative character of the abstract intellect in its under-standing of nature. The truth is that the process of conversion yielding this intellect undergoes a most remarkable shift even while following the straightforward line of identification. The real abstraction arises in exchange from the reciprocal relationship between two commodity-owners and it applies only to this interrelationship. Nothing that a single commodity-owner might undertake on his own could give rise to this abstraction, no more than a hammock could play its part when attached to one pole only. It is purely owing to the interlocking of the exchanging agents in the reciprocity of their claims – their 'do ut des' – (I give that you may give) – that the act of exchange assumes its abstract nature and that this abstraction endows exchange with its socially synthetic function. To apply the exchange relation to Robinson Crusoe in his dealings with the nature surrounding him, as bourgeois economists are so fond of doing, removes all trace of the real abstraction from what they call 'exchange'. Yet, strangely enough, when the real abstraction has finally been converted into the conceptual structure of the abstract intellect, we are faced with a relationship not so far removed from that of Robinson to nature, for this intellect applies itself to external reality in accordance with the familiar subject – object pattern of the relationship of cognition. The relational shift is so complete that it seems to make an absurdity of our contention that such a contrast is the result of nothing more devious than a process of successful identification. And yet on closer scrutiny it can be seen that this complete change of scenery, if I may thus describe the relational shift, is an integral and inevitable part of the very process of the conversion.

We clearly saw that the real abstraction inherent in exchange becomes discernible only in coined money. In any previous commercial practice still compatible with communal forms of society (in fact interspersed throughout the Near and Eastern Mediterranean orbit with remnants of such forms) the real abstraction was, of course, equally operative but in a way absolutely concealed from the human mind. The introduction and spread of coinage, however, ousted communal production and heralded a form of social synthesis rooted in 'reification', so called because the social context of people is transformed into the social context of their products intercommunicating in the monetary terms of their prices, their 'commodity language' as Marx puts it. We shall return to these historical aspects of our subject in Part II of this book. Coined money operates as the functional intermediary of the social synthesis. The commodity-owners no longer refer to each other, but to their money. Thus only at the advanced stage of reification prevailing in commodity production at its full growth do the conditions arise where the conversion of the real abstraction into conceptual terms becomes a possibility. And under these conditions the elements of the exchange abstraction present themselves to the human mind, one single mind every time, as properties of objects which in fact relate to nature, not to money.

(c) CONVERSION *POST FESTUM* OF EXCHANGE (MARX – 'AFTER THE EVENT')

In the first place it must be reiterated that the conversion of the exchange abstraction does not take place as a part of commercial activities. For its commercial purposes coinage is perfectly adequate in its empirical state as made of metal or its substitutes. The discrepancy between the actual coinage and the exchange abstraction cannot leave its mark on people in the bustle and fray of the market but strikes them only as a matter for contemplation and mental reflection.[34] Here we enter into the cognitive relationship of subject to object and the object within this relationship stands for nature. For, in the second place, we must be clear as to the precise contents of the exchange abstraction. These contents are nothing but the basic features of the physical act of commodity transfer between private owners. It is this physical event which is abstract (this is precisely why we have called it the 'real abstraction'). It is a compound of the most fundamental elements of nature such as space, time, matter, movement, quantity and so on. The concepts which result from the identification of these elements are thus in their origin concepts of nature. Between them, they constitute an all-encompassing pattern or framework of nature in the abstract. In logical terms they can be described as non-empirical, purely formal concepts of timeless universality. And they can relate to nothing other than to a nature seen as physical object-world antithetically divided from the social world of man and from its history. The world of the concepts based on the exchange abstraction is the same as that criticised by Marx in a famous footnote of *Capital*, vol. 1, where he speaks of 'the abstract materialism of natural science, a materialism that excludes the historical process'.[35]

(d) DIVISION OF SOCIETY AND NATURE

What happens at the formation of this non-human object world of nature is a peculiar turnabout of the emerging intellect at the concluding point of the conversion. While the non-empirical concepts which make up the intellect's impersonal equipment wipe out every trace of its social origin and cause it to stand, as it were, with its back to society, these same concepts turn into instruments of cognition facing the external reality of nature. For by their abstractness from all sense reality of use the concepts also lose all human reference and retain non-human nature as their only content.

Conceptual reasoning emerges in a process which causes an impenetrable self-alienation of the abstract intellect and at the same time, endows it with a capacity of logical self-direction. Once the elements of the real abstraction have assumed conceptual form, their character, rooted in social postulate, evolves into the dialectic of logical argument attached to the concepts. The argument concerns the application and the interpretation of the concepts, as either right or wrong, correct or incorrect. Thus the Parmenidean τὸ ἔον referring, according to our contention, to the material that coinage *should* be made of, but is not and cannot be made of, become prescriptive of the correct way to reason about reality. And this correct way as a general rule will conform to the make-up of the existing social formation based on commodity production. The reasoning itself, however, is totally impervious to this conformity since its alienation blinds it to society. This creates the division of society and nature which emerges with commodity production and outdates the anthropomorphic blending characteristic of the communal forms of society preceding commodity production.

Francis Cornford gives a telling example of such an anthropomorphism when he quotes Sophocles from *Oedipus Rex*: 'So, ... when a sin has been committed – such as the unconscious incest of Oedipus – all Nature is poisoned by the offence of man. The land of Thebes "Wasteth in the fruitless buds of earth, In parched herds, and travail without birth of dying women".'[36] As George Thomson puts it: 'In primitive thought, society and nature had been one. Thales and Anaximander succeeded in separating nature from society and presenting it as an external reality existing independently of man. Similarly, Solon succeeded in separating society from nature and presenting it as a moral order based on obligations peculiar to man. In other words, just as Anaximander objectified nature, so Solon objectified society.'[37]

(e) REIFICATION AT THE ROOT OF THE INTELLECT

It may be confusing to be told that the notion of nature as a physical object-world independent of man emerges from commodity production when it reaches its full growth of monetary economy. Nevertheless this is a true description of the way in which this conception of nature is rooted in history; it arises when social relations assume the impersonal and reified character of commodity exchange. We saw that in exchange the action is social whereas the minds are private, and that it is the physical action of the commodity transfer between the owners which is abstract. The action of exchange stands in antithetic polarity to the sense-reality of things in the private minds of the individuals in their social life. The non-empirical concepts drawn from the real abstraction describe that action reduced to bare-bone physical reality. It is a reality carrying universal social validity among all exchanging agents. These concepts have objective reality in application to natural events because they relate to form categories of physical events, of a kind which could be described as the absolute minimum of what can constitute a natural event, for they are events which happen while the material status of things undergoes no change. They constitute the paradigm of mechanistic thinking. Its concepts are, in their origin, the forms of the act of commodity exchange, and in their content the basic categories of nature as object-world in antithetic contrast to man's own social world. The content of these concepts bears absolutely no reference to money. Their only trait relating to money and to exchange is their abstractness. The abstractness itself is the work and outcome of exchange, but this fact is completely unrecognisable to any mind or 'intellect' using these concepts. Such an intellect is bound to be alienated by false consciousness when it tries to explain its own mode of thinking.

The self-explanation assumes the materialistic or the idealistic variant according to whether its basic concepts are recognised as non-empirical or as derived from external reality. Non-empirical concepts cannot be explained in materialistic ways – that is, by way of direct reflection – and idealism is thus at an epistemological premium regardless of its blatant absurdities otherwise.

(f) KNOWLEDGE FROM SOURCES OTHER THAN MANUAL LABOUR

Owing to the concepts drawn from the exchange abstraction the intellect is equipped with instruments of cognition which, if employed in a suitable method, can yield a knowledge of nature from sources totally alien to manual labour. It is a knowledge ruled by a logic of appropriation, or, more precisely, by a logic of the reciprocal appropriation which rules in the market, as opposed to manual production. A logic of production could only be the logic of producers for the pursuit of their production, individually or in common. It would be a logic of unity of head and hand, whereas the logic of the market and of mechanistic thinking is a logic of intellectual labour divided from manual labour. Therefore, the concepts deriving from the exchange abstraction – that is the concepts of mechanistic thinking – we may term as 'original categories of intellectual labour'. It is a labour serviceable to the rule of private property and in particular to capital.

It is the science of intellectual labour springing from the second nature which is founded upon non-empirical abstraction and on concepts of an *a priori* nature. The form elements of the exchange abstraction are of such fundamental calibre – abstract time and space, abstract matter, quantity as a mathematical abstraction, abstract motion, etc. – that there cannot be a natural event in the world which could elude these basic features of nature. They make up between them a kind of abstract framework into which all observable phenomena are bound to fit. Anything descriptive of this framework such as, for example, the geometry of homogeneous space, would be applicable to such phenomena with *a priori* assured certainty, although, of course, in a manner appropriate to the specific properties of the phenomenon concerned. While these properties in their infinite variety are conveyed through sense-perception and are as accessible to manual producers as to scientists, the conceptual issues are the exclusive prerogatives of the intellectual workers. It is this theoretical part which holds the epistemological problems. The main one among these attaches to the understanding of nature by its laws; to the possibility and conditions of such understanding.

(g) LAWS OF NATURE

The discovery of natural laws was the set objective of the mathematical and experimental method of exact science as understood and practised in the classical Galilean – Newtonian era. The rise of modern science ran parallel with the rise of modern capitalism. In Part II of this study we shall analyse their formal and inherent connection; at present we are concerned to clear up the epistemological issue of science as raised by Kant, with whom we have one important point in common. Kant argued with great vigour and with a polemical edge against English empiricism that the discovery of natural laws presupposes the employment on non-empirical concepts such as, say, the concept of inertial motion as defined by Newton in his 'first law of motion'. On the other hand, it is extremely difficult to see how such a concept, just because it is non-empirical and cannot be gleaned from nature or supplied by the practice of experience, could possibly give access to the inner workings of nature far beyond sense-perception. It was this contradiction which prompted Kant to turn the tables on all previous epistemological standpoints and to decide that, as the concepts of science could not be assumed to be modelled on nature, the only way to account for the facts of Newtonian science was to postulate that nature, or rather our human kind of experience, was modelled on the non-empirical concepts of our pure understanding. Now Kant was driven to this conclusion because he could not imagine that non-empirical concepts could possibly have natural or historical, or in any case spatio-temporal, roots. The same holds true for all philosophical materialists. To their minds anybody believing that non-empirical concepts play a vital part in science must be an idealistic thinker. Conversely, anybody resolved to adhere to his materialism is committed to hold mistaken ideas about ancient and bourgeois science. Our study is calculated to remedy this paradoxical situation. For we show that non-empirical concepts are not necessarily beyond the reach of materialistic explanation. We are therefore in a position to dismiss both these philosophies, idealist and materialist, and to follow historical materialism as our only methodological guide-line.

(*h*) THE GUIDE-LINE OF HISTORICAL MATERIALISM

Marx contemplated human history as a part of natural history, a tangential part, as it were, which takes shape in the protracted process by which man succeeds in producing his own means of livelihood. This holds a promise that man will eventually assume control of his historical destiny, but until that stage is reached the development of mankind is the result of blind necessity and is as much a working of natural history as, say, the generation of a new biological species would be in non-human nature. But the difference is that history, by being channelled through human society, brings forth mental rather than physical alterations in man, developments like language, conscious reflection, faculties of knowledge together with those of error and human self-delusion and even possibly also of a social self-realisation of man. True, the nature from which the non-empirical categories of intellectual labour are drawn is not the primary nature of physical reality but the second, purely social nature which, in the epochs of commodity production, constitutes a vital part of that 'social being of men which determines their consciousness'.

However, the very categories which constitute second nature are products of man's natural history. Commodity exchange, when attaining the level of a monetary economy, gives rise to the historical formation of abstract cognitive concepts able to implement an understanding of primary nature from sources other than manual labour. It seems paradoxical, but is neverthe-less true, that one has first to recognise the non-empirical character of these concepts before one can understand the way in which their indirect natural origin through history achieves their validation. One might speak of science as a self-encounter of nature blindly occurring in man's mind.

(i) MONEY AS A MIRROR OF REFLECTION

To trace the natural origin of such categories in this historical manner, or rather to develop them historically from their social roots, is well in keeping with the method advocated by Marx. In a much-quoted footnote in *Capital*, vol. 1, he calls this method 'the only materialist, and therefore the only scientific one'.[38] I deem it superior to the theory of reflection especially in regard to concepts of basic importance in intellectual labour divided from manual labour. Reflection, however it may be interpreted and differentiated, must be the activity of bodies with individual senses and individual brains, whereas abstract intellectual labour relies from the outset on terms of logical uniformity and universality. The contrast of approach and specificity of understanding can be brought out clearly by attempting to interpret our theory in terms of the theory of reflection. The role played by money and coinage in mediating the formation of the purely intellectual concepts according to our explanation can be likened to the part played by a medium of reflection. The real abstraction of exchange is reflected in coinage in a manner which allows intellectuals to identify it in its distinct elements. But first of all, the reflection itself is not a mental process; second, it is on a social scale; third, it is hidden to the consciousness of the participants; and, fourth, it is associated with the formation of false consciousness. How could necessarily false consciousness be admitted as the medium for the reflection of truth or of true reflection?

(j) THE SOCIAL FORM OF THINKING

The fact that the reflecting medium of the real abstraction is coinage accounts for the creation of logical uniformity of the intellectual abstraction among all conceptual thinkers in an exchange society of a given stage and formation. But it does more than that. The basic categories of intellectual labour, we have seen, are replicas of the elements of the real abstraction, and the real abstraction is itself that specific characteristic which endows commodity exchange with its socially synthetic function. Therefore, intellectual labour, in employing these categories, moves in the mould of the formal elements of the social synthesis. The social synthesis is the rationality of intellectual labour in its scientific activity; in classical antiquity this included philosophy. Scientific work, its conceptual or theoretical part, if correctly done is socially valid, not only because it rests upon a community of thinking among the intellectuals. It would have social validity even if it stood on lonely ground and met with the disagreement of everybody else in the existing confraternity of intellectuals and scientists. Throughout the ages of commodity production, from its initial form of ancient slave society to its ultimate capitalist completion, the products of manual labour are private property whereas the products of intellectual labour are social property. If an individual mind conforms to the elements of the real abstraction, by which society itself forms a functioning network and an economically viable system, then this mind is by itself capable of producing socially valid results. For this mind acts intellectually for society. In fact it does so in a 'super' capacity, much as society would itself act as an entirety if it were equipped with the necessary body and brain. Instead it uses individual minds as its representatives. Such a mind then acts as the only one of its kind, excluding a plural in the same way as society and money cannot be more than 'single' at any time. A closer analysis would reveal that the 'transcendental unity of the self-consciousness', to use the Kantian expression for the phenomenon here involved, is itself an intellectual reflection of one of the elements of the exchange abstraction, the most fundamental one of all, the form of exchangeability of the commodities underlying the unity of money and of the social synthesis. I define the Kantian 'transcendental subject' as a fetish concept of the capital function of money.

As it assumes representation as the *ego cogito* of Descartes or of the 'subject of cognition' of philosophical epistemology the false consciousness of intellectual labour reaches its culmination: the formation of thinking which in every respect merits the term 'social' presents itself as the diametrical opposite to society, the EGO of which there cannot be another. Kant has the appropriate formula for this contradiction: 'There is no ground in theoretical reason from which to infer to the existence of another being.' Nothing could be wrapped in greater secrecy than the truth that the independence of the intellect is owed to its originally social character. Science is equipped for its socially necessary tasks, but only with false self-awareness. 'Science', here, is understood as divided from manual labour.

(k) THE SOCIAL SYNTHESIS AS THE FOUNDATION OF SCIENCE

From the results so far we can draw the general conclusion that, within the limits of commodity production, the valid foundations of the science of an epoch are those in keeping with the social synthesis of that epoch. We shall see that significant changes in the formation of the social synthesis indeed entail corresponding changes in the formation of science.

We limit this conclusion to the epochs of commodity production. 'Objects of utility become commodities only because they are the products of the labour of private individuals who work independently of each other.'[39] This statement of Marx indicates the reason why a society based on this mode of production is in need of intellectual work by social thinking and why social thinking must be divided from physical labour. Physical production has lost its direct social cohesion and can form a viable totality only by the intermediary of a network of exchange under the rule of private property. As capital it controls production. In a variety of ways – by slave labour, serfdom or wage labour – it subjects manual labour to exploitation. The manual labour becomes impoverished, not only economically because of its exploitation, but also intellectually. Individual labour is in full control only in the small-scale individual production of peasants and artisans. Only then is production based on the individual unity of head and hand. This artisan mode of production is ousted by capitalist production initially by nothing more than a larger size changing its scale to the social one of 'simple co-operation' in the Marxian sense of this term. Not infrequently this enlarged scale was necessitated by the novel and special nature of the production task.

Social history first embarked on commodity production with the beginning and development of Iron Age technology from the times of Greek antiquity onwards. It progressed slowly, culminating in modern capitalism where commodity production became the all-pervading form of production to the extent that practically no product whatsoever can any longer be produced except as commodity. Yet, right up to the end of the nineteenth century the productive forces at the disposal of mankind must still be classed as those of the Iron Age. This means that the basic pattern of commodity production, marked by the separation of the activities of physical work and the activities of social interrelationships (i.e. exchange) remains unchanged. But with the rise of monopoly capitalism around the turn of the century the pattern began to show modifications and there occurs a change of science and technology which marks a transformation of the productive forces into those of atomic physics and of electronics. These transformations will occupy us in Part III of this volume but the consequences are so novel and so enormous that nothing more than question marks, at best intelligent ones, can be within our scope.

PART II

SOCIAL SYNTHESIS AND PRODUCTION

10

Societies of Production and Societies of Appropriation*

We have already made mention of the factor by which the conditions of production within class societies differ from those of classless ones. The contrast hinges on the different nature of the social synthesis. If a society has the form of its synthesis determined by the labour relationship in the production process, thus deriving its fundamental order directly from the labour process of man's acting upon nature, then the society is, or has the possibility of being, classless. We have spoken of such societies under Marx's term 'communal modes of production'. Labour is either done collectively by members of a tribe, or if done individually or in groups the workers still know what each one does, and work in agreement. People create their own society as producers. The structure enables us to call them 'societies of production'. The alternative is a form of society based on appropriation.

We understand appropriation as functioning between men within society, as the appropriation of products of labour by non-labourers; not, as sometimes described, as man appropriating his needs from nature. Here we must differentiate between unilateral and reciprocal forms of appropriation. Unilateral appropriation of the surplus product leads to the manifold forms of a class society which Marx called 'direct lordship and bondage'. The appropriation here is carried out by the imposition of tributes, forced or voluntary, or by plain robbery; it is carried out as a public activity by the rulers and can be based on subjugation or on 'god-given rights'. But the questions which interest us attach

---

* In this part, as elsewhere in the book, we shall limit ourselves in the main to the broader aspects of historical understanding without dealing with them in detail.

to forms of society based on reciprocal appropriation as private exchange; in other words, to the various forms of commodity production. The common feature of all societies of appropriation is a social synthesis effected by activities which are qualitatively different and separated in time from the labour which produces the objects of appropriation. It is unnecessary to stress that no social formation, whether based on production or on appropriation, can be understood without due consideration of the productive forces in their particular state of development.

In Part I of this book we attempted to show that a social synthesis effected through the reciprocal forms of appropriation in commodity exchange leads to the inception of intellectual labour of a kind separated from manual labour. From this one might be tempted to generalise and to conclude: whatever the social formation, be it one of appropriation or production, the socially synthetic functions will determine the forms of consciousness of its epoch. If this generalisation proves true our analysis might gain significance for our present concern in the struggle for socialism.

I I

Head and Hand in Labour

First of all it must be stated that no human labour can take place without a degree of unity of head and hand. Labour is not animal-like and instinctive, but constitutes purposeful activity; the purpose must guide the physical endeavour, no matter what kind, to its intended goal as a consequential pursuit. Marx writes

> We presuppose labour in a form in which it is an exclusively human characteristic. A spider conducts operations which resemble those of the weaver, and a bee would put many a human architect to shame by the construction of its honey-

comb cells. But what distinguishes the worst architect from the best of bees is that the architect builds the cell in his mind before he constructs it in wax. At the end of every labour process, a result emerges which had already been conceived by the worker at the beginning, hence already existed ideally.[1]

But for us the essential question is: in whose head is the intended result of the labour process anticipated?

In so far as the labour process is purely individual, the same worker unites in himself all the functions that later on become separated. When an individual appropriates natural objects for his own livelihood, he alone supervises his own activity. Later on he is supervised by others.[2]

Of course, in one special sense, as work carried out as a one-man job, the individual labour process stands at the beginning of commodity production, but not at the beginning of human history. It must thus be decided whether the intended achievement of a labour process is an idea in the head of a single performer, or of several collectively, or whether it might lie in an alien head which deals the workers mere snippets of the process which signify to them no end goal whatsoever. Dependent on these alternatives are the changes in the relationship between head and hand, the relation between intellectual and manual labour.

It is important for us to differentiate between personal and social unity, or division, of head and hand. Personal unity attaches only to the labour of the one-man producer. This does not mean that, conversely, all individual one-man production presupposes such a personal unity; for example the slaves who produced the pottery or textiles by their individual labour were far from being masters of its purpose or form. Personal division of head and hand applies to all labour whose purpose is prescribed elsewhere. Social unity of head and hand, however, characterises communist society whether it be primitive or technologically highly developed. In contrast to this stands the social division between mental and manual labour – present throughout the whole history of exploitation and assuming the most varied forms.

Viewed as a whole, the development of society moves historically from primitive communism where production is totally communal, step by step to the extension of individual one-man production covering every essential area and thus to the beginning of commodity production. At this stage the use of coinage heralds the epoch of the social form of thinking as separate pure intellect. Manual production becomes single production, but at the same time intellectual labour becomes universalised. This middle stage of the historical development was reached in classical antiquity and produced societies of appropriation in their absolute 'classical' form; that of Roman and Greek slave labour where the slave does not partake in human society. But from the breaking up of this epoch a process begins where socialisation seizes upon production and even upon manual labour itself, thus pushing forward to today's stage of development. Now, within the capitalist society of appropriation, the preconditions of a modern society of production have ripened and, as Marx and Engels predicted, mankind is face to face with the ineluctable alternative of a society of production, or a society of appropriation. My intention is to follow through the main stages of this whole development in the most compressed form.

12

The Beginnings of Surplus Production and Exploitation

By this title we understand the transition from the primitive, communistic society of production to the first forms of society of appropriation. The beginnings of appropriation within society presuppose a growth in productivity or a development in the productive forces of collective communal labour sufficient to expect regular surpluses of a worth-while dimension over and above subsistence level. As Marx puts it:

> It is only when men have worked their way out of their initial animal condition, when therefore their labour has been to some extent socialised, that a situation arises in which the surplus labour of one person becomes a condition of existence for another.[3]

The first beginnings of appropriation develop within the community and bring with them slow but nevertheless incisive changes in the conditions of production based on communal property and consumption. Marx recognises a particular phenomenon as necessarily mediating these changes; namely, the rise of exchange with other communities, an exchange having an erosive feed-back effect on the order of things within. A more permanent effect arises when those who benefit from the incipient appropriation become active forces driving on the development in their own interests and organising themselves into a separate social power. Their influence prompts increasing incursions into the communal property, particularly of the land, with growing conditions of dependency for the producers. Gradually there crystallise hard-and-fast class divisions within the society, based on inheritance, patriarchy, wars of conquest and extensive plundering and trade.

This brief outline is designed to bring out three fundamental factors: In the first place the primary producers, tillers of land, cattle-rearers, etc., remain for a long time communal; second, the enrichment of the appropriating class occurs in the forms of unilateral appropriation of the surplus product; third, the exchange of products maintains, for the most part, the character of external trade between different communities. It is only later that exchange develops into the form of the inner social nexus.

Individual production started at its earliest with the making of stone tools and weapons, but continued in the artisan crafts of later Neolithic inventions such as in secondary production like pottery, spinning and weaving, mainly by women; then towards the end of the Neolithic Age in the metal crafts which were the work of men. The secondary industries became the main area of trade, just as trade became the promoting force for the growth of the secondary crafts. The production of surplus and the class-character of wealth underwent a massive impetus through the development and interaction of these two factors, secondary industries and trade, and so set in motion such an incredible achievement as the cultivation of the great fertile river valleys, which, from the Nile to the Yellow River occurred within the same time span, between the fifth and third millennia B.C.

13

Head and Hand in the Bronze Age

Not before the development of iron metallurgy did individual, small-scale farming become the method and the standard of primary production; and between the Neolithic and the Iron Ages lie thousands of years, the millennia of the Bronze Age. This epoch had its own characteristic social formation, that of the ancient oriental cultures which, from the cultivation of the fertile river valleys, appear as large-scale civilisations compared with the preceding Neolithic communities. For our particular sketch, ancient Egypt will serve as a model, for it is here that the first preliminary forms of the division of intellectual from manual labour appear at their clearest. It is generally recognised that later Greek philosophy and science were heavily indebted to this epoch.

The ancient oriental social formation had the character of a two-story structure. The base comprised agriculture and animal husbandry on the fertile land and its surroundings, an economy which we can sum up under the name of alluvial primary production. This was still carried out by the methods of collective communal production relying on stone tools and not on metal implements, because bronze was far too precious to be put in the hands of the cultivators.[4] In other words the communal character of the form of production was not dissolved. The fertility of the alluvial soils was preserved and increased by the skilful and methodically planned irrigation systems more or less common to all these civilisations, thus drawing from primary production a surplus which was vast measured by earlier standards.

The occupation and clearance of the river valleys was not done by the producers on their own initiative, but under the whip and direction of the rulers either of the same or another ethnic origin. From the very beginning their purpose was to appropriate the increased surplus product. This extraordinary achievement in itself presupposes a decisive division between the dominating and organising rulers and the physical exertions of the collective primary producers. The delivery of the surplus product by the producers or alternatively its collection by the rulers and their functionaries necessitated hardly any additional coercion. It was a result, by and large, of the reverential obedience of the producers to their rulers. The Pharaoh was the supreme owner of the cultivated land, and through his supposed sacred relationship with the powers of nature guaranteed the producers lasting possession of the soil and the very possibility for their pre-servation. The appropriation was public and official activity centred in the Pharaoh whose whole State was organised as a machine for the collection, storage and disposal of the surplus. This does not exclude the existence of exchange and trade, but it was carried on as external state trade with foreign communities.

Based on the appropriation of the vastly increased surplus, a culture now developed which formed the second story of the social formation. This employed the crafts of Neolithic origin to serve the exclusive and qualitatively highly refined needs of the rulers. The metallurgy of bronze and of the precious metals takes first place in these crafts, as in all probability the foundation and achievement of the whole culture would have been impossible using only stone tools. For the furtherance of these secondary crafts, including textiles, woodwork, rope-making, stone-cutting, jewellery, cosmetics, sculpture and so on, there unfolds a far-flung trade where the primary products, conserved and stored in chambers and granaries, were exchanged for the raw and auxiliary materials necessary for the luxury production. It was a trade carried out with other States and communities by order and in the name of the Egyptian State, and in addition benefited their immense building projects and cult activities, state-organised mines, expeditions and war campaigns. The exchange trade, however, did not permeate the internal order of these Bronze Age societies.

This whole upper story of the civilisation rested, in direct 'lordship and bondage', on the unilateral appropriation of the primary surplus product. And it was to promote this appropriation and its actual performance, that script and the art of writing, numeration and arithmetic – in other words symbolic forms and separate intellectual labour came to be conceived and developed. Thus, in our opinion, intellectual in separation from manual labour arises as a means of the appropriation of products of labour by non-labourers – not originally as an aid to production. It served the calculation of tributes, the accounting of credits and repayments in the relation between the temple authorities or officials of the Pharaoh and their debtors, the storing and listing of appropriated products, the recording of the volume of incoming or outgoing supplies and other similar operations.

A good illustration is provided by the reports and surmises of Herodotus about the origins of geometry in ancient Egypt. Rope was its principal tool and 'geometry' was practised as a professional skill by people whom the Greeks, translating the Egyptian name literally, called 'harpedonapts': stretchers of the rope. The teaching and exercise manual of Ahmes found in the Rhind Papyrus together with numerous Egyptian reliefs show clearly that these stretchers of the rope were assigned, usually in pairs, to the high officials of the Pharaoh for the building of temples and pyramids, the laying down and paving of dams, the construction of granaries and measurement of their volume, and, most important, to parcel out the soil afresh when it re-emerged after the dispersal of the yearly floods of the Nile. This could evoke the impression that geometry had been invented for the sake of the cultivators – that is, in the relation of man to nature – rather than out of the social production relations and the economy, as Marx would lead one to expect. In actual fact, however, many of the Greek historiographers were inaccurate and incomplete in their presentation, for in the text of Herodotus he says specifically that this partition of the soil was done for the purpose of reassessing the peasants' tributes for the coming year. Hence geometry did not appear to the cultivators in their own garb but in the attire of the Pharaoh's tax officials accompanied by their field measurers.

If the rope was handled with the necessary dexterity and with the know-how of long experience one can reasonably suppose that there were few problems of geometry that this technique could not successfully overcome. Among its achievements were the tripartition of angles, the magnification and dimunition of volumes including the doubling of cubes and finally even the calculation of the constant pi which Ahmes puts at 3·164. That this exercise of 'geometry' could only aspire to approximations, even if at times it achieved amazingly accurate ones, is self-evident, but a claim to 'mathematical accuracy', had this concept existed, would perhaps have seemed mere pedantry to these 'geomatricians'. Rope-stretching was a technique of measuring, nothing more, but it involved great skill and yielded a practical use-value as high, if not higher, than that of the geometry of the Greeks. According to all appearances it found acceptance in ancient India too, the earliest textbook of Indian geometry bearing the very title *The Art of the Rope*. There also was a special cultivation of the art of counting by means of the abacus and thus there unfolded in that country through two or more thousand years an art and knowledge of geometry and of numbers which astounded Europe when the Arabians began to make themselves the Islamic propagators of both traditions in the eighth and ninth centuries A.D. Joseph Needham has shown that in China there was a similar mathematical knowledge as elsewhere in the Far East.[5]

The mystery of the Egyptian calendar and of the astonishingly accurate calculation of the year and of the Nile floods have been robbed of much of their aura by modern research. According to the studies of Siegfried Schott[6] and Richard A. Parker[7] the alleged sun calendar of Egypt was in reality merely a moon calendar adapted by purely empirical interpolation to what was observed of the orbit of Sirius. The fabulous capabilities of the Egyptians in astronomy are thus reduced to proportions more in keeping with the rest of their proven intellectual practice. The mystification inherent in this astronomy was, however, no error, but was the wily intention of the priests. The benefit to class rule of the mere appearance of the division of head and hand far preceded its real development. One knows of the artificial magic created by the priests to play on the credulity of the masses. Their wizardry went to the extent of bringing their figures of gods and goddesses alive by the action of steam from boiling vessels which was led through long underground pipes to the altar, so that the gods appeared to open their eyelids and their mouths and to let off steam in their anger. Thus a make-belief of division of head and hand prevailed in the service of class rule, and long preceded the reality.

The textbook of Ahmes preserved on the Rhind Papyrus in the British Museum consists of a collection of simple tasks for practical purposes – for instance, of the way to calculate the number of bricks required for the covering of an irrigation dam of a given height and length and slope – and for each of these tasks the pupil is given instructions on how to proceed. Even the concept of a theorem lies on a level of abstraction too high for this kind of 'mathematics', whose very characteristic is the lack of the logical foundation and systematic coherence by which it later assumes its intrinsic division from manual labour. It is true that intellectual and manual labour was already divided into acti- vities of different people and, more important, of separate castes and classes conscious of the distance between each other. But mental labour did not yet possess the intellectual independence which severs it inherently from manual labour without the need of caste divisions or mystifications.

Our particular interest now centres on the reasons why, at the ancient oriental stage of social formation, the division of intellectual from manual labour lacked an inherent foundation. The base of this formation differed from that of commodity production by the unilateral appropriation operated by the rule of direct 'lordship and bondage'. Its economic context can be likened to that of a huge state household (as Marx puts it) planned and calculated to its finest detail.

But however different this practice of unilateral appropriation may have been from the relation of commodity exchange, it contained certain important features in common with the abstract function of the exchange relation. The action of appropriation, just like that of exchange, was most strictly separated in time and place from any use of the appropriated objects. The products were stored and quantified without any change to the state in which they were delivered by the producer and accepted by the appropriator. Moreover, the unchanged substance of the objects of appropriation were not classified under the same terms as were the objects of use or labour. But even without a detailed form analysis of one-sided appropriation – which is not the same in ancient oriental as in medieval feudalism – the essential differences from commodity exchange are obvious. He who performed the action of appropriation (official of the Pharaoh, priest, scribe) did not act on his own initiative or for his own benefit. He collected the objects but did not deliver them. The man who did deliver them was not his personal debtor. The appropriator was only the functionary of a superior total power, one single link of an entire, complex, extensive hierarchy in the service of this power. He saw, not the whole appropriation, but only one particular part at a particular place, and of a particular kind. But even within a specific product it was not the whole of the kind, not all the barley, not all the corn which was the object of appropriation but only the surplus part of it, the other part of the same product remained in the possession of the producers and played quite a different role in the total order of existence. In short, nowhere in this order is a generality reached which is applicable to all its objects or subjects. The objects of appropriation certainly possess an identity as value; of this their accounting, the economy of the system, offers direct proof – but this economy has no generality in substance nor in function.

However, it is important to understand that precisely those factors which prevent a generalisation of value and of form determination make it possible for the total order to be controlled, comprehended and governed. The thought of the system's functionaries lacked rationality in theory to the same degree as the system possessed rationality in practice. This is only the converse of the observation already made that the 'autonomous intellect is an effect of the exchange mechanism through which man loses control over the social process'. Ancient oriental economy was a planned economy, its irrationalities were not of a kind to make its order uncontrollable.

Thus the results of our survey are twofold. First, the intellectual development which took shape in the Bronze Age occurred in that sphere of social formation based on appropriation separated from production. Second, this intellectual development had not yet achieved any intrinsic division from manual labour because appropriation controlled only a part of the social product and therefore did not constitute the general form of the social synthesis. The division between intellectual and manual labour can only occur when appropriation assumes the reciprocal form of private exchange when the object of appropriation takes on commodity form; or, alternatively, when individual small-scale production spreads to include primary as well as secondary production. This did occur in the epoch of iron metallurgy when cheap metal tools became available to the primary producers, making them independent of the cumbersome and extensive collective irrigation economy of the alluvial river valleys. Incidentally their individual labour became more productive than the communal economy of any previous epoch.

14

The Classical Society of Appropriation

The new iron metallurgy which emerged onwards from around 1000 B.C. brought about the civilisations of the Phoenicians and then of the Greeks, the Etruscans and the Romans. These civilisations required far less space for food production than their predecessors; they could populate hilly country, coastal strips and islands and gain advantages from their mobility. In order to produce a surplus of their primary production with iron implements they were no longer dependent upon the cultivation of alluvial river soils. The legends of their heroic early phase prove that they waged raids of destruction, plunder and abduction in the fabulously wealthy territories of the ancient oriental Bronze Age civilisation. In the process they acquired the superior craftsmanship and techniques of these older civilisations. They soon caught up and even overtook their predecessors in secondary production and particularly in the making of weapons and building of ships.

The individualisation of production that now emerged is reflected in the fact that these adventurers indulged their deeds of robbery and pillage on their own account and at their own risk; they were no longer in the service of theocratic rulers or backed by the power of a whole State. They acted as heroes, independent individuals, with whom their people and State could identify, devoting themselves in this way to their particular function, the appropriation of existing alien wealth. Their mythological frame of reference is still related to that of the Bronze Age civilisations except that the gods are transformed from what were, in effect, legitimations of the appropriators in the image of a higher power into deities guarding the destinies of the heroes themselves. Here one sees the nucleus of private wealth and of commodity exchange before this exchange leads to the emergence of money.

The social revolution brought about by the development of the iron technique is summed up by George Thomson in the following words: 'by increasing productivity and so rendering possible new divisions of labour, the use of iron carried still further the process of transforming collective production and appropriation into individual production and appropriation. Hence it marked a new stage in the growth of commodity production. The village commune, resting on common ownership and surrendering its surplus in the form of tribute, was succeeded by a community of individual proprietors, each producing independently for the open market. Such was the Greek *pólis*, based on the use of iron.'[8]

Engels follows Lewis Morgan in seeing developed commodity production as synonymous with the first stage of civilisation, which he describes as follows: 'The first stage of commodity production with which civilisation begins is distinguished economically by the introduction of (1) metal money, and with it money capital, interest and usury; (2) merchants, as the class of intermediaries between the producers; (3) private ownership of land and the mortgage system; (4) slave labour as the dominant form of production.'[9] I would also add that the first stage of civilisation is not only distinguished economically, but that the division of intellectual and manual labour becomes a factor of prime importance.

The chief difference between ancient and capitalist commodity production was that the producers remained owners of their means of production. When, in fact, they lost this ownership they fell into slavery, and became the means of production themselves in person, *possessed* by their slave-owner. The wealth acquired by slave-owners and by the landed aristocracy was either by unilateral appropriation by means of tributes, rents, war booty and loots, or by such methods in addition to commerce. Thus occurred a more or less violent redistribution of possessions and property, with a disruptive impact upon the traditional communal and tribal forms of society. The formation of wealth, all of it in terms of substantial riches of jewellery, precious objects, palaces and so on took place through *external* relations between 'barbarian' or other Greek communities by means of trading, warfare or colonisation. Only when the commercial element grew so dominant that it resulted in the first invention of coinage on the Ionian side of the Aegean around 680 B.C. did the disruptive effects transfer themselves to the *internal* order of the home community. Engels's description of this process is so powerful and so instructive that it is worth quoting at some length:

> Towards the end of the upper stage of barbarism, . . . through the sale and purchase of land, and the progressive division of labour between agriculture and handicraft, trade and shipping, . . . the smooth functioning of the organs of the gentile constitution was thus thrown so much out of gear that even in the heroic age remedies had to be found. [There followed the division of] the entire people, regardless of gens, phratry or tribe . . . into three classes: nobles, farmers and artisans. . . . The power of the nobility continuously increased, until about the year 600 B.C. it became insupportable. And the principal means for suppressing the common liberty were – money and usury. The nobility had their chief seat in

and around Athens, whose maritime trade, with occasional piracy still thrown in, enriched them and concentrated in their hands the wealth existing in the form of money. From here the growing money economy penetrated like corrosive acid into the old traditional life of the rural communities founded on natural economy. The gentile constitution is absolutely irreconcilable with money economy; the ruin of the Attic small farmers coincided with the loosening of the old gentile bonds which embraced and protected them. The debtor's bond and the lien on property (for already the Athenians had invented the mortgage also) respected neither gens nor phratry, while the old gentile constitution, for its part, knew neither money nor debts in money. Hence the money rule of the aristocracy now in full flood of expansion also created a new customary law to secure the creditor against the debtor and to consecrate the exploitation of the small peasant by the possessor of money. All the fields of Attica were thick with mortgage columns. . . . The fields not so marked had for the most part already been sold on account of unpaid mortgages or interest, and had passed into the ownership of the noble usurer; . . . and that was not all. If the sale of the land did not cover the debt, . . . the debtor had to sell his children into slavery abroad. . . .

The rise of private property . . . led to exchange between individuals, to the transformation of products into *commodities*. And here lies the seeds of the whole subsequent upheaval.

But the Athenians were soon to learn how rapidly the product asserts its mastery over the producer when once exchange between individuals has begun and products have been transformed into commodities. With the coming of commodity production, individuals began to cultivate the soil on their own account, which soon led to individual ownership of land. Money followed, the general commodity with which all others were exchangeable. But when men invented money, they did not think that they were again creating a new social power, the one general power before which the whole of society must bow. And it was this new power, suddenly sprung to life without knowledge or will of its creators, which now, in all the brutality of its youth, gave the Athenians the first taste of its might.[10]

There is no doubt that this complete social revolution must have been associated with its own appropriate form of thought. We have explained how the exchange abstraction can become the basis of a complete mode of thinking when exchange assumes the role of the social nexus. George Thomson has not only confirmed and supported the study of Engels, but has carried the enquiry to greater depths and new results. 'From Ionia the new medium spread across the Aegean to Aegina, Euboea, Corinth, Athens, and a little later to the Greek colonies in Italy and Sicily. Thus Greek society was the first to be based on a monetary economy. The significance of this development has seldom been appreciated.'[11] George Thomson, like myself, links the rise of commodity production in Greece with the rise of Greek philosophy.

I make a differentiation between primitive exchange on the one hand and private commodity exchange on the other. The former was contemporary with the various forms of 'communal modes of production' and evolved chiefly in the external relations between different tribal communities. Its beginnings preceded the development of the exploitation of man by man and in fact helped to promote the progress of the productive forces preconditional to the rise of such exploitation. In its initial stages, as we have described by the example of ancient Egypt, exploitation took the shape of systems of direct lordship and bondage. When the productive forces developed further by the transition from Bronze to Iron Age communal food production was superseded by individual production combined with an exchange of a new kind, the private exchange of 'commodities'. 'Commodities' then answered the Marxian definition as 'products of the labour of private individuals who work independently of each other'.[12]

This kind of exchange – commodity exchange properly speaking – is the one which is characteristic of Greek antiquity. It leads to a monetary economy and to a system of social synthesis centred on private appropriation. Whereas in the system of direct lordship and bondage, as in Egypt, appropriation is public and relates to production, here appropriation is private in such a way that one act of appropriation relates to a reciprocal counteract, both linked under a postulate of equality. This constitutes a network of social synthesis entirely in terms of property. Production is done by chattel slaves who are owned by their masters as their personal property and who themselves do not take part in that network of property, having no access to money.

Here we have the social system of reification governed by the anonymous rule of the exchange abstraction. The contrast between the proto-intellectual labour of the Bronze Age and the real intellect is vividly stated by Benjamin Farrington

> with the Greeks a new and most important element did enter science. This is the element of speculative philosophy, which constitutes the specific quality, the real originality, of Greek science; . . .
>
> The organised knowledge of Egypt and Babylon had been a tradition handed down from generation to generation by priestly colleges. But the scientific movement which began in the sixth century among the Greeks was entirely a lay movement, it was the creation and the property, not of priests who claimed to represent the gods, but of men whose only claim to be listened to lay in their appeal to the common reason in mankind. The Greek thinker who advanced an opinion stood behind the opinion himself. He claimed objective validity for his statements; but they were his own personal contribution to knowledge and he was prepared to defend them as such. Consequently with the Greeks individual scientists begin to emerge, and the specific quality of scientific thinking begins to be recognised.
>
> To put the matter in another way, the world-view of the Egyptians and Babylonians was conditioned by the teaching of sacred books; it thus constituted an orthodoxy, the mainten-ance of which was in the charge of colleges of priests. The Greeks had no sacred books, . . .
>
> Thales [born about 630 B.C., who founded the Early Ionian School] is the first man known to history to have offered a general explanation of nature without invoking the aid of any power outside nature.[13]

Too little is known of the historical details of the beginnings of the conceptual mode of thinking for us to be certain of the social class of its main protagonists. Significant, however, is its place of origin. Miletos, on the Ionian coast of the Aegean Sea was the foremost centre of the commercial activity and colonial expansion of the Greeks in the eastern Mediterranean down to Nauplia in Egypt, north to the Black Sea and as far west as Massalia, the present Marseilles. Thales himself was, according to Herodotus, partly of Phoenician descent and belonged to an ancient family of priest-kings, as also did his contemporary Anaximander, perhaps the greatest of the Ionian philosophers. Thales, in addition to his interests in science, technology, philosophy and geometry, was also reputed to have organised a corner in oil and pursued other commercial activities.

By the end of the eighth century, as George Thomson records, the Greeks had broken the Phoenician monopoly of the Aegean carrying-trade and were challenging them in the Levant.[14] From the same century chattel slavery developed, and the Milesian merchants were selling slaves from the northern colonies to Egypt and Syria in the seventh century. Early in the eighth century the traditional rule of the landed aristocracy had been overthrown, following which Miletos itself was shaken by political upheavals and alternating regimes of tyranny and democracy. From the end of the seventh century the city-state suffered two generations of civil war.

George Thomson sums up ancient Greek history in these words:

> The truth is that, just because they were based on small-scale production, the Greek city-states, having grown up in conformity with the new developments in the productive forces, especially iron-making and the coinage, were able, under the democracy, to insinuate slave labour surreptitiously into all branches of production, and so create the illusion that it was something ordained by nature. It was then that 'slavery seized on production in earnest' [Marx]. This was the culmination point in the evolution of ancient society, to be followed by a long decline, in which the limitations inherent in the slave economy asserted themselves on an ever-increasing scale, obstructing the further development of the productive forces and diverting the energies of society from the exploitation of nature to the exploitation of man.[15]

I5

Mathematics, the Dividing-line of Intellectual and Manual Labour

In Chapter 13 we illustrated the proto-intellectual character of the mental work in the Bronze Age by describing the Egyptian geometry of the rope. We found it to be a highly efficient and multivariant art of measuring attaining useful and indeed astonishing grades of approximation. But it was in the character of a skill rather than of a science even though it depended on extensive geometrical interpretation and instruction as indispensable accessories to manual practice.

Admittedly, from my perspective, I would not place traditions handed down from the Bronze Age or even earlier on the same level as the mathematics created by the Greeks. They replaced the rope by ruler and compass and thus transformed the previous art of measurement so fundamentally that something completely new grew out of it – mathematics as we understand it. The geometry of the Greeks is of a purely intellectual character and detached from the practice of measurement. How could the change in the implementation achieve such a difference, or, rather, what transformation occurred to bring this change about?

The art of the rope was a manual skill which could only be carried out by those apprenticed to do it and practised in it and only at the particular spot where the need for measurement arose. Divorced from this it had no point. Neither did it leave behind any detachable demonstration of its geometric content. After each action of measurement, each 'measure', the rope was moved on from one position to another so that such a thing as a direct 'geometrical demonstration' never came into question. The geometry inherent in the task at hand extinguished itself in the practical result, which was only ever applicable to the case in point. To be sure, the 'harpedonapts' in the course of their training had to be taught and shown the constantly recurring elements in their techniques and with Ahmes much of this is presented in the guise of geometric rules. But it must surely be nothing but a reflex of our own conceptions when mathematical historians (including Moritz Cantor, Sir Thomas Heath and D. F. Smith) conjecture that a theoretical manual must have existed serving as a foundation to Ahmes's book of practical exercises – a manual which has never been found.

The Greeks, however, invented a new kind of geometric demonstration. Instead of stretching ropes, they drew lines by ruler which remained on the sheet underneath, and together with more straight lines, formed a permanent figure from which could be recognised geometric laws. The combination of lines were tied to no particular location, and their size was infinitely variable.

The geometry of the measurement thus became something quite different from the measurement itself. The manual operation became subordinated to an act of pure thought which was directed solely towards grasping quantitative laws of number or of abstract space. Their conceptual content was independent not only from this or that particular purpose but from any practical task. In order, however, to detach it from such application a pure form abstraction had to emerge and be admitted into reflective thought. We reason that this could result only through the generalisation intrinsic in the monetary commensuration of commodity values promoted by coinage.

It goes without saying that this radical transformation from the Egyptian art of measuring to the geometry of the Greeks did not occur at one stroke, but only over hundreds of years and mediated by incisive developments to the productive forces and by corresponding changes in the relations of production. For proof of this one need go back no further than to the beginnings of Greek geometry. The invention which bears Thales's name is traditionally connected with the measurement of distance of ships from the coast; here the art of the rope would clearly have been useless. This one example illustrates the world-wide difference between the Bronze Age mainland economics of

Egypt and Mesopotamia based on agrarian exploitation, and the Greek city-states based on sea-voyaging, piracy and trade. The Greek forms of production were peasant agriculture on a small scale, and independent handicrafts. The new monied wealth of the Greeks emanated solely from the circulation nexus, an achievement effected, as Lenin says, by merchants' and usurers' capital. It did not spring from the land or from the workshops of manual producers, at least not before these were replaced by slaves, who themselves became the source of commodities for exchange.

An essential point regarding the 'pure mathematics' of the Greeks is that it grew to be the unbridgeable dividing-line between mental and manual labour. This intellectual significance of mathematics is a central theme with Plato. Euclid, in his 'Fundamentals of Geometry', created an imperishable monument to it at the threshold of Hellenistic culture. This work seems to have arisen for the sole purpose of proving that geometry as a deductive thought structure was committed to nothing but itself. In the synthetic quality of thought no account was taken of the material interchange of man with nature either from the point of view of the sources and means involved, nor from that of its purpose or use. Into this glasshouse of Greek thought went 'not a single atom of natural matter' – quite parallel with commodities and their fetish identity as 'value'. It was the pure formalism of 'second' or 'para-'nature and suggests that in antiquity the form of money as capital, in other words the functionalism of second nature, finally remained sterile. Although it had indeed freed labour from slavery it had failed to lower the reproduction cost of human labour power in any noteworthy way, if at all. We can conclude this to be true in retrospect from the fact that development after Euclid by Archimedes, Erastosthenes, Apollonius, the legendary Heron and many others, in whose mathematical elements of abstract dynamics were already noticeable, consequently achieved technical application limited only to military or other wasteful ends.

16

Head and Hand in Medieval Peasant and Artisan Production

We can sum up by saying that the salient feature of antiquity in our context is that the social category of value as money and as capital – capital operating solely as merchants', usurers' and predatory capital – failed to communicate its social character to labour. Labour was not human labour; it was slave labour, a variant of animal function. Any co-operation performed under the whip of the slave-driver ceased when the slaves were freed. As a freed man the individual dropped out of any co-operation, both the one involved in slavery and also the co-operation within the tribal community to which he belonged before his enslavement. The end-result of the ancient forms of commodity production was the final dissolution of the numerous forms of communal production which preceded it or were initially coexistent with it. The description we quoted from Engels of the dissolution of the Athenian gentile society only exemplifies the process which took place throughout the length and breadth of the Roman Empire until it reached its own dissolution. In fact, ancient commodity production economically fed on the very process of dissolving primitive tribal economies and came to an end of its monetary economy when there were none of these left to dissolve. Rome then became a place inhabited by an atomised mass of about two million individuals living on unemployment benefit and social security, as we would say today, to supply them with '*panem et circenses*' – food and entertainment – rather than using the payment to organise production – capitalist production as it would have been. Production was supplied by the enormous latifundia run on slave labour and owned by the senators and 'equites' ruling the Empire. As the economy lost its character of a monetary and slave economy it transformed into feudalism which represented the final legacy Rome bequeathed to its medieval successors.

The negativity of the Roman decline, the disintegration of the ancient formation of commodity production, brought forth a positive result of great importance: the humanisation of labour. By this I mean that productive labour lost its incompatibility with the human quality of man and could be undertaken without the risk of enslavement. 'Christianity with its religious cult of man in the abstract'[16] was a plausible ideological exression of this innovation. The serf and the villain were baptised the same as the feudal lord, and from the very start this religion sought its converts partly among the slaves and the freedmen, but mainly among people of the labouring and the artisan status.

The economic development in European feudalism started again with 'peasant agriculture on a small scale and production of independent artisans, both of which, on the one hand, form the basis of the feudal mode of production' as they had also formed 'the economic foundation of the communities of classical antiquity at their best, after the primitive oriental system of common ownership of land had disappeared and before slavery had seized on production in earnest'.[17] It is almost as though history was making a restart after the communal modes of production had been cleared out of the way and labour freed from slavery. We shall note later (p. 110) how this restart led on to a road which took mankind in a direction diametrically opposed to that of the first start.

The advantage that feudalism offered to the humanised labour of the small-scale peasant and artisan producers lay in the fact that the means of labour was made available to them notwithstanding that they were dependent on the lords who owned the land. The individual production proceeded on the lines of a division of labour within the economic framework of the medieval manor. In the undivided possession of their physical and mental capabilities and left to the freedom of their inventiveness for the sake of lightening their work these small-scale producers achieved an enormous increase of productive capacity through the massive utilisation of the natural forces of water, wind and beasts of burden.

The draught-power of horse and ox was revolutionised by the invention of the breast-strap harness, making possible the use of the heavy plough; stirrup and iron horseshoes were developed and means of transport increased and improved so as to bring corn, wood, wool, dyer's woad, etc., to the watermills and later to the windmills for processing. These mills were used in a multitude of ways and were connected with the invention and improvement of new tools and methods of work. No room is available here for the relevant and interesting details. A good indication of the development, however, is contained in the Domesday Book of 1086 which enumerates no fewer than 5624 watermills south of the Trent and Severn. Of outstanding importance for subsequent developments was the progress in animal rearing and particularly of sheep breeding for wool processing.[18]

This general growth of the productive forces available to the individual peasants and artisans, between the ninth and thirteenth centuries, gave rise to a change in the mode of feudal exploitation. The appropriation of the surplus assumed forms which, while more successful in enriching the feudal exploiter, were at the same time more apt to give greater mobility and scope of initiative to the exploited. It was the era of the formation of towns and of growing expansion of monetary relationships. It was followed in the next two centuries by a mounting trend towards the emancipation of economic developments from the tentacles of feudalism. In the words of Rodney Hilton: 'the history of the English agrarian economy in the 14th and 15th centuries illustrates very well the consequences of successful peasant resistance to the lords' pressure for a transfer of surplus. In fact, it must be regarded as a critical turning point in the history of the "prime mover". [of the social change in progress – S-R] The long period of the successful and multiform exploitation of peasant labour ended, at any rate in most Western European countries, between the middle and the end of the 14th century.'[19]

However, the era of a free peasant and artisan economy was not long-lived. It did not survive the fifteenth century. To the degree to which the emancipation succeeded, the direct producers retained their technical independence of choosing what and how to produce, but by no means their freedom from economic exploitation. They exchanged the bonds of feudal tyranny for the entanglement of the ever-tightening net of the merchants' and usurers' capital. Again to quote Rodney Hilton: 'Moneyed wealth, which was not based on the possession of landed property, came from trade, which was in the hands of monopoly companies of merchants like the Merchant Adventurers and the Merchants of the Staple.'[20]

The developments described here with special, although by no means exclusive, reference to England took place much earlier in Flanders and Italy, particularly in Florence which is, of course, of primary importance from our point of view. In the thirteenth century the struggle for urban independence and emancipation from the forces of rural feudalism was led everywhere by merchant capitalists and bankers. But in the towns this went hand in hand with the growing exploitation and impoverishment of the producers whose character as artisans gradually deteriorated to that of mere cottage labourers.

Feudalism has grown out of the declining Roman economy; now the rise of merchant capital led to the revival of a monetary economy, thereby linking up, so to speak, with the point where the economy of antiquity had given up. Proof of this is found in many places, but nowhere with greater clarity than in England. Here, around A.D. 900 monetary economy had already begun, not as a result of such pervasive trade relations as that of Italy with Byzantium and the Levant but for the very different and more local reason that the Danes, on their second invasion of England's east coast, had imposed upon the king the payment of a tribute in money. As a consequence the king was forced to establish a monetary accountancy. By the twelfth century one finds detailed instructions for the running of the royal exchequer and the collection of tax in cash, thereby enforcing monetary thinking upon the taxpayer. Some two hundred years later, in Oxford, manuals were compiled with exact and varied material for teaching bailiffs, reeves, accountants and other administrators of feudal domains from the perspective of loss and gain. These have recently been published in an admirably painstaking edition by Dorothea Oschinsky under the title *Walter of Henley and other Treatises on Estate Management and Accounting*.[21]

The earliest of these texts is by Robert Grosseteste (died 1253), bishop of Lincoln, who advises the Countess of Lincoln on how to make bigger gains and fewer losses on her very numerous manorial estates. In 1214 the same Grosseteste became the first Chancellor of the colleges of Oxford, and thus founder of the university. His significant achievements as an academic make him the earliest in that succession of great Oxford scholastics, whom one might even call English Aristotelians, including such names as Roger Bacon (1214–95), Duns Scotus (1270–1308), Thomas Bradwardine (1290–1349) and William of Occam (1295–1350). These scholastics maintained a constant exchange of ideas and comings and goings between Oxford and Paris.

The close ties between the monetary and the scholastic developments are obscured by a peculiar state of affairs. The educational books for the profitable administration of feudal estates had to be written in the French of that time instead of in Latin so as to be understood by the Norman overlords, and for this reason were excluded from the records of the university, although this whole branch of teaching took place in Oxford. The historians of the university know nothing of it, and in most cases it is not even known who were the authors of the manuals. But scholasticism's connections with its economic background can be recognised on quite a different level: from the perspective of money on the one hand and from that of labour and production on the other. The first new mathematical developments took place from 1202 onwards when Leonardo da Pisa published his *Liber Abaci*. This innovation in mathematics was again associated with a change of implementation. The Greeks excelled in geometry but not in arithmetic and algebra although they possessed and used the abacus. The Indians, the Chinese and later the Arabians combined the technique of the abacus with a rational numerical notation which took them far ahead of classical antiquity.

About Leonardo of Pisa's *Liber Abaci* Moritz Cantor writes: 'Despite its total mathematical clarity and discipline, it was offputtingly difficult. On the other hand it dealt with things which the merchant could use in the demands of daily life and sometimes had to.'[22] Cantor tells how Leonardo's father, himself a merchant of Pisa, demanded that his son 'devote several days to the study of the abacus'. He was introduced to this discipline by the help of the Indians' nine numerals, found pleasure in it, and on trade journeys which he later undertook to

Egypt, Syria, Greece, Sicily and Provence learnt everything there was to know about this practice of counting. But this 'everything', together with Algorism and the segments of Pictagoras [sic], 'seemed to me as so many errors compared with the method of the Indians'. And he had specialised in the Indian method, added things of his own, enriched the geometrical art of Euclid by new subtleties and so published his work in fifteen sections – all 'so that the race of Latins' (meaning the Italians) 'should no longer be found ignorant in these matters'.

The 'demands of daily life' of the merchants was that of great international trade which, at the time of the Crusades, joined together European feudalism with the Arabian and Byzantine empires. It was a trade for which Leonardo and others taught methods of calculating the purity content of precious metals since the international standard coins such as the gold florin, the ducat, the sequin and the guilder went into circulation only when feudal domination had collapsed after the death of Frederick II in 1250. From that date the independence and rise of the towns depended only on the towns themselves and on their internecine rivalries. This dating may be too precise since the developments depended on the uneven progress, not only between North and South, but, more important, of the manufacture of cloth (the principal commodity of international trade) centred in Flanders and northern Italy on the one hand and the wool-producing countries of England, Spain, France and Saxony on the other.

By 1350 (a hundred years later) the commercial activities of merchant capital had already developed so extensively that the production relations were rapidly changing. The supplying countries and particularly England began their own cloth manufacture. Up to then the Italian and Flemish buyers, for example, had negotiated most of the wool deliveries with the domain managements; now, however, the greater part of the wool-supplies was contracted by individual, direct producers who gained their independence from the domains, enlarged their flock of sheep, and began to enjoy a growing monetary income, the feudal lords leasing them the necessary pasture land. In England wool became the commercial equivalent for money, and Edward III (1327–77) frequently accepted tax payments in wool in lieu of money. (Hence the Woolsack of Parliament.) The historical events leading to the later Enclosure Acts date back to this time. There occurred the transference of monied wealth to a growing middle class of agrarian and artisan stock who themselves had changed from the labourers employed by feudalism to employers of labourers producing for merchant capital. The end of the fourteenth century sees the transition from artisan modes of production to the pre-capitalist epoch – the epoch of the Renaissance with which the history of the development of natural science begins.

Here the development, moving in a diametrically opposite direction to ancient commodity production, of which we spoke at the opening of this chapter, started to take shape. Whereas the originally social character of labour with which human history begins reached the point of absolute dissolution in the decline of the Roman Empire when its slave economy changed to feudalism, now, as medieval feudalism ends, the trend of renewed co-operation of labour in production occurs under the impact of the merchant-capitalist developments. This trend inaugurates the epoch of pre-capitalism from around 1300 onwards until two and a half or three centuries later the situation is rife for merchant-capitalism to turn into production-capitalism; that is to say, into capitalism proper. But the important difference of the renewal of the socialisation of labour from its primitive counterpart is that the modern form feeds entirely on the resources and incentives of the second nature and no longer on those of primary nature. It no longer depends on the standards and the capacities of the direct material interchange of man with nature, but on the subordination of labour to capital.

17

The Forms of Transition from Artisanry to Science

Medieval handicraft began with the personal unity of head and hand; Galilean science established their clear-cut division. In this chapter we are concerned with the transition from artisanry to science from this viewpoint. The causes of the transformation can be found in the change from one-man production to production on an ever-increasing social scale. This occurred, as we have seen, mainly as a result of the commercial revolution.

The formation of towns as urban communities started in the era of late feudalism. With their development sprang the need for communal walls, communal defences, communal town halls, cathedrals, roads and bridges, water-supplies and drainage systems, harbour installations and river control, monuments and so on. These were all due to the activities of capital, commercial and monetary, 'antediluvian forms of capital', as Marx calls them. The social character of all this development is the direct outcome and manifestation of the originally social power of capital. Under this power the great mass of the artisans were ruthlessly exploited. They still retained the status of producers owning their own means of production, but the bulk of them did so as impoverished cottage labourers, hopelessly indebted to the capitalist for whom they produced the merchandise. They were downgraded and depressed to the standard of proletarian labour long before they actually assumed the status of mere wage-labourers. Production taking place in artisan workshops, on the other hand, increased in volume and changed in labour methods. The employment of more *and* more semi-skilled workers resulted in class divisions within the workshops.

From our viewpoint, however, these economic and sociological changes are not the main focus of interest. They are not the
ones that can explain the logical and historical steps leading to
the formation of science. Parallel to the economic developments
making for the eventual dissolution of the artisan mode of
production go technological changes caused by the increasingly
social scale of the order of life as a whole exemplified by the town
developments.

Construction and production tasks of such dimensions and
novelty stretched the craftsmen to the limits of their resources and
inventiveness. By the necessity to tackle the problems there rose
from the ranks of ordinary producers the great Renaissance
craftsmen, the 'experimenting masters', artists, architects, and
also engineers of the fifteenth and sixteenth centuries. The main
qualification which the craftsmen lacked in their capacity as
artisans for solving the problems facing them can be named in
one word – mathematics. We have defined mathematics as the
logic of socialised thought. Capital and mathematics correlate:
the one wields its influence in the fields of economy, the other
rules the intellectual powers of social production.

We must be clear about the limits that are set to the capacity of
work tied to the personal unity of head and hand. The artisan or
individual manual worker masters his production, not through
abstract knowledge, but by practical 'know-how' and by the
expertise of his hands. In terms of 'knowledge', it is the
knowledge of how one *does*, not of how one *explains* things. This
practical knowledge can be conveyed by demonstration, repetition or words, depending on practical understanding of the
task involved. Cookery books are a clear example. This is,
moreover, not only true of human functions. Let us suppose we
deal with working a pump, a threshing-flail or a water mill,
irrespective of whether they replace human labour or whether
man cannot perform their task. In speaking to manual workers
one could not express oneself in any other way than by treating
these things as if they took the part of human agents. The
language of common usage (devoid of special technical terms)
cannot articulate a division of intellectual and manual labour.
The only symbol language which rends itself free from this tie-up
with human activity is that of mathematics. Mathematics cuts a
deep cleft between a context of thought and human action,

establishing an unambiguous division of head and hand in the production processes.

It is no exaggeration to say that one can measure the extent of division of head and hand by the inroad of mathematics in any particular task. More than any other single phenomenon it was the development of firearms which imposed the use of mathematics on artisanry. Needless to say, the technology of firearms did not cause the dialectic of the precapitalist development, but from the second half of the fifteenth century it intensified and accelerated technological developments enormously. The use of firearms was confined to guns for artillery, and in this capacity created problems completely new and alien to artisan experience and practice – problems such as: the relationship between the explosive force and the weight of cannon and range of fire; between the length, thickness and material of the barrel; between the angle and the resulting path of fire. Metal-casting assumed new proportions, as did the mining of ore, the demands of transport, and so on. Special importance accrued to military architecture for the defence of cities and harbours. From the fall of Constantinople to the Turks in 1453 well into the sixteenth and even seventeenth century the Turkish menace hung over Europe like a nightmare. After the fall of Otranto in the Adriatic in 1490 Venice felt under the threat of immediate assault and in 1532 the Turks laid siege to Vienna.

To gauge the strain and stresses which the urgency of this turn of events laid upon European artisanry would demand a study beyond our scope. We can, however, gain an illuminating insight into the contradictions of the epoch by drawing upon the writings of Albrecht Dürer (1471 – 1528) as a master in both the arts and mathematics. My remarks are based on *Instructions of Measurement with Compass and Ruler* (1525)[23] and on the *Instruction as to the Fortification of Town, Castle and Hamlet* (1527). Here the unique attempt is made to refashion mathematics to make it a fitting discipline for the use of artisanry. This means, of course, to attempt the impossible. Nevertheless his venture was so significant that it occupied mathematicians and military architects of the whole of the sixteenth century and to some extent up to the eighteenth century.

Dürer had studied mathematics at the highest academic level of that time with his learned friends in Nuremberg, Willibald

Pirckheimer and Johann Werner. Instead, however, of using this knowledge in its scholarly form he endeavoured to put it to the advantage of the craftsmen. The work is dedicated to 'the young workers and all those with no one to instruct them truthfully'. It aims to change geometry by modifying its implements; he replaces the ruler by the set-square and alters the use of the compass by restricting it to a fixed aperture. According to generally accepted surmise Dürer, for this, drew on the tradition of workshop practice and in particular of that of the mason lodges. What is novel in his method is that it tries to combine workmen's practice with Euclidean geometry, and to reconcile these two seemingly incompatible elements by aiming at nothing more than approximate results sufficient for practical needs. He writes: 'He who desires greater accuracy, let him do it *demonstrative*, not *mechanice* as I do it.'

As Moritz Cantor points out: 'Albrecht Dürer is the first to apply the principle of approximation with full awareness.' Only in his construction of the pentagon does Dürer neglect this distinction, presumably because he takes it to be accurate, albeit erroneously. 'The fact that he otherwise makes such a clear distinction between what is correct and what is of practical use places him on a plane of science reached by hardly any other geometrician of the 16th century.'[24]

On the subject of Dürer's construction of the pentagon Leonardo Olschki writes:[25] 'The construction of the regular pentagon by this method [the fixed-compass aperture – S.-R.] exercised the wits of such mathematicians as Tartaglia, Cardano, G. del Monte, Benedetti and others, until finally P. A. Cataldi devoted a special dissertation on it which appeared in Bologna in 1570.' He was a member of the Florentine Accademia del Disegno, where twenty years later Galileo also taught. Galileo too dealt with Dürer's construction in his lectures on military architecture of 1592–3, and even Kepler, in his *Harmonices Mundi* (1619), still discussed Dürer's construction of the septagon.[26]

What Dürer had in mind is plain to see. The builders, metal workers, etc., should, on the one hand, be enabled to master the tasks of military and civil technology and architecture which far exceeded their traditional training. On the other hand, the required mathematics should serve them as a means, so to speak, of preserving the unity of head and hand. They should benefit by the indispensable advantages of mathematics without becoming mathematical brainworkers themselves; they should practise socialised thinking and yet remain individual producers. And so he offered them an artisan's schooling in draughtmanship, permeated through and through with mathematics (not to be confused in any way with applied mathematics). Nothing can illustrate the inner paradox of the pre-capitalist mode of production more clearly than this attempt of Dürer's; nothing can so illuminate the interrelationship of the intellectual form development with the economics of the conditions of production than its fate. It met with failure on both counts.

To do justice to the inner nature of this achievement of Dürer is impossible here. Two or three quotations must suffice to illustrate it. His stereometric constructions in the Fourth Book of the *Instructions of Measurement* end: 'Here I have drawn up everything quite openly after which I closed it, laid it on the ground and opened it up once more.'[27] In numerous constructions he points out ways in which they could prove useful to his work-mates; here, for instance, with the doubling of the cube: 'In this way they could duplicate, triplicate and infinitely increase and augment the cube and all other things. Now as such an art is of great use and serves the end of all workmen but is held by all the learned in the greatest secrecy and concealment, I propose to put it to the light and teach it abroad. For with this art, firearms and bells can be cast . . . barrels, chests, gauges, wheels, rooms, pictures and what you will, enlarged. Thus let every workman heed my words, for they have never, to my knowledge, been given in the German language before this day.' From the squaring of circle: 'Mechanice, that is approximately, so that at work it will fall short of nothing or of very little, and could be put by comparison as follows. . . .' Regarding approximation: 'Now I shall change a previous triangle into a septangle through a common trick which we need to speed up a job of work.'

But, in fact, Dürer's intentions came to nothing because he demanded far too much in the way of mathematical understanding from the apprentices and craftsmen of his time despite all the painstaking efforts he had taken to be sufficiently explanatory. Moreover, his aims to save the unity of head and hand were frustrated by the response that his writings evoked from the subsequent mathematicians mentioned above. They never considered, for instance, the geometry of fixed-compass aperture as a means of helping the craftsmen. Their main effort was directed towards demonstrating that this geometry could cope with the entire body of the Euclidean geometry, its principles, theorems, problems and all. Hence Dürer's was not a particular artisan geometry; indeed, such a geometry does not exist and cannot be invented.

This re-establishment of mathematics as the dividing-line between head and hand is all the more conclusive as Tartaglia himself copes with artisan problems. In his book of 1537 and the first eight books of the second one of 1546 as well as in a number of his 'risposte' (replies) to Ferrari he deals with questions of ballistics, harbour fortification and cannon-casting which the highly skilled craftsmen of the Venice arsenals had put to him as their mathematical consultant. And in parts of his own work Tartaglia also uses the geometry of fixed-compass aperture. In his case it is as difficult, as in Dürer's, to be sure where this geometry, attracting such wide interest throughout the sixteenth century, had its origin. The most likely assumption is that it answered the requirements of the Venetian craftsmen as Dürer's did the demands of those of Nuremberg. Tartaglia, however, charged a fee to the workmen for the answers he gave them – indeed it was the main source of his living – and showed no sign of wanting to bolster up their education.

Tartaglia and his pupil Benedetti and their enemies Cardano and Ferrari, as well as Cavalieri and the other Italian mathematicians of the sixteenth century, already trod upon early capitalist ground. They worked for the steady deepening of the cleavage between head and hand and groped towards the science whose methodological basis is the completed severance of the one from the other.

18

The Capitalist Relations of Production

The Italian mathematicians we mentioned were the immediate forerunners of the scientific revolution. It is our endeavour to understand the historical and logical genesis of the exact sciences as an essential part of the capitalist relations of production. Our first need to this end is a clear conception of what exactly is involved in the relational change from the artisan mode of production to the capitalist.

The artisan producer owned his means of production, but in the fifteenth and sixteenth centuries his economic independence had been so undermined that it became all but fictitious that they were his own property. However, so long as his means of production had not actually been taken from him, no matter how heavily they were pledged to the capitalist, we still move in the era of the production relations of artisanry. The artisan nominally sold his finished product to the merchant. As long as this was the case the responsibility for the process of production, the quality, the quantity, the manner and date of delivery rested with the artisan producer. As a consequence the manner of production and of its physical conditions were still conceived in terms of artisanry and these were basically terms of the unity of head and hand of the artisan in person. He performed small-scale production on the basis of personal skills, and, like an artist, judged things by his senses.

Now let us assume for argument's sake that the merchant capitalist, who had hitherto been satisfied to 'buy' his wares from the artisan producers, decides instead to seize the means of production, the workshop, implements and materials and to carry on production by employing the artisans as wage-labourers. There is nothing to stop him legally, materially or economically from doing so, since financially these things have long been forfeited to him already. Thus the capitalist acquires the direct control of the labour process and assumes the status of 'producer' or, as we say by an even worse misnomer, the status of 'manufacturer'. By this change of production relations the responsibility for the production process in all its material aspects and conditions has shifted from the direct producer to a social power which does not partake in the process of production by one single physical function of its own. In what terms have we, then, to conceive of the responsibility of the capitalist for the process of production under his control? This question allows for a concise answer: the control of capital over production must be entirely in terms of second nature, and of second nature in both representations – the real abstraction in the economic field and the ideal abstraction in the intellectual field of science. On both levels the terms of the second nature are, we have seen, totally 'abstract' from the empirical realities of use, either consumption or production, and they are alienated from all contact and interchange with the first nature. Our main concern in this study is the shaping of the ideal abstraction, but we cannot broach our subject adequately before making a brief characterisation of the material basis.

How does the capitalist perform his role of 'producer'? He performs it not by way of labour, not with his hands, not by tools or machines which he operates. He performs it with his money which he uses as capital and with nothing else. To exercise his role of 'producer' the capitalist must be able to buy everything on the market; materials, land, services, labour and know-how, which, correctly assembled under his command at the right place and time, constitute a labour process in which he himself, the capitalist, never need lay a hand. 'The labour-process is a process between things the capitalist has purchased,' says Marx, 'things which belong to him.'[28] If, indeed, he should have to put his hand to the wheel it would merely prove that he had failed in his function as a capitalist and entrepreneur, and, strictly speaking, he should pay himself for his own manual labour. In other words the role of producer now falls on a person who does not perform a single productive function in the labour process. From the perspective of the capitalist entrepreneur the essential characteristic of the production process for which he is responsible is that it must operate itself. The controlling power of the capitalist hinges on this postulate of the self-acting or 'automatic' character of the labour process of production. This all-important postulate of automatism does not spring from any source in the technology of production but is inherent in the production relations of capitalism.

However, a postulate is not necessarily a reality. It becomes a reality only when the appropriate conditions exist for its practical realisation. The change from the handicraft to the capitalist mode of production did not occur suddenly in the sharply defined manner our description might suggest. Even during the actual period of transition in the sixteenth century the change took place gradually and in a great variety of ways. Marx has given an unforgettable picture of the violence, cunning and ruthlessness of its methods in his account of the so-called primitive accumulation. Our presentation has been reduced to a formalisation only for theoretical purposes.

In its initial stage the capitalist mode of production suffered from many imperfections. By rights the capitalist should find the factors he needs for his production process available in the market. But throughout the sixteenth, seventeenth and eighteenth centuries this was far from the case. The capitalist had therefore to be his own inventor, his own engineer and master craftsman and often enough even his own labourer. The workmen available for employment were originally the same artisans who had worked for the craftsmen of the pre-capitalist workshops. Although they still worked with hand-tools they differed from the producers of the preceding era by becoming increasingly subject to such close division of labour that they were crippled artisans and mere 'detail labourers' as Marx calls them. It was only under the pressure of the severest managerial authority that they were forced to act as pawns to the capitalist producers instead of remaining producers themselves.

In few other parts of *Capital* does Marx discuss the phenomenon of capitalist management in such detail as in the chapter on the manufactural stage of capitalist production, concluding his analysis of Manufacture with the following:

During the manufacturing period proper, i.e. the period in

which manufacture is the predominant form taken by capitalist production, the full development of its own peculiar tendencies comes up against obstacles from many directions. Although . . . manufacture creates a simple division of the workers into skilled and unskilled at the same time as it inserts them into a hierarchical structure, the number of unskilled workers remains very limited owing to the preponderant influence of the skilled. . . . Since handicraft skill is the foundation of manufacture, and since the mechanism of manufacture as a whole possesses no objective framework which would be independent of the workers themselves, capital is constantly compelled to wrestle with the insubordination of the workers. 'By the infirmity of human nature', says our friend Ure, it happens that the more skilful the workman, the more self-willed and intractable he is apt to become, and of course the less fit a component of a mechanical system in which . . . he may do great damage to the whole.' Hence the complaint that the workers lack discipline runs through the whole period of manufacture. . . . During the period between the sixteenth century and the epoch of large-scale industry capital failed in its attempt to seize control of the whole disposable labour-time of the manufacturing workers, and . . . the manufactures are short-lived, changing their locality from one country to another with the emigration or immigration of workers. . . . At a certain stage of its development, the narrow technical basis on which manufacture rested came into contradiction with requirements of production which it had itself created. . . .' This workshop, the product of the division of labour in manufacture, produced in its turn – machines. It is machines that abolish the role of the handicraftsman as the regulating principle of social production. Thus, on the one hand, the technical reason for the lifelong attachment of the worker to a partial function is swept away. On the other hand, the barriers placed in the way of the domination of capital by this same regulating principle now also fall.[29]

Once the dominion of capital finds an objective basis in the employment of machinery the previous ambiguities in the position of the labourers are swept away and Marx explains:

Every kind of capitalist production, in so far as it is not only a labour process but also capital's process of valorization, has this in common, that it is not the worker who employs the conditions of his work, but rather the reverse, the conditions of the work employ the worker. However, it is only with the coming of machinery that this inversion first acquires a technical and palpable reality. Owing to its conversion into an automaton, the instrument of labour confronts the worker, during the labour process in the shape of capital, dead labour, which dominates and soaks up living labour-power. The separation of the intellectual faculties of the production process from manual labour, and the transformation of those faculties into powers exercised by capital over labour is . . . finally completed by large-scale industry erected on the foundation of machinery.[30]

Judging from our experience with contemporary industry the 'conversion into an automaton' not only seizes upon the single instruments of labour, but affects entire factories as integrated complexes of machinery and labour. To reiterate the chief point: the tendency which I described as the 'postulate of automatism' presents itself as a feature of technology. But it does not spring from technology but arises from the capitalist production relations and is inherent in the capital control over production. It is, as it were, the condition controlling this control.

This postulate of automatism clearly stands in diametrical contrast to the principles of handicraft and to the whole manner of thinking associated with the artisan's mode of production. As long as handicraft plays any essential role in the capitalist labour process, as during the seventeenth, eighteenth and even the early nineteenth centuries, automatism will not take full command. Handicraft acts as a stop-gap, if not as a hindrance to capital, exercising its own specific kind of control. During the Industrial Revolution, when machinery came to play a more and more predominant part, all important machine tools were inventions of craftsmen, even though their work shows a tendency to science, and so does the production process itself. As Marx expresses it:

This subjective principle of the division of labour no longer exists in production by machinery. Here the total process is examined objectively, viewed in and for itself, and analysed into its constitutive phases. [Disregarding the remaining elements of handicraft] A system of machinery . . . constitutes in itself a vast automaton as soon as it is driven by a self-acting prime mover. . . . As soon as a machine executes, without man's help, all the movements required to elaborate the raw material, and needs only supplementary assistance from the worker, we have an automatic system of machinery. . . . An organised system of machines to which motion is communicated by the transmitting mechanism from an automatic centre is the most developed form of production by machinery.[31]

However, this fully developed form of the capitalist factory was not realised before the second half, or even the last third, of the nineteenth century after the technique of producing machines by machines had been well mastered. Thus the introduction of machinery in the second phase of development of the capitalist mode of production, the phase marked by the Industrial Revolution was not only motivated by the drive for a higher rate of exploitation and a lowering of production costs, but also by the need for 'a framework apart from the labourers themselves' for the control of the labour process. The postulate of automatism as a condition for the capital control over production is even more vital than its economic profitability – it is fundamental to capitalism from the outset.

A capitalist enterprise may survive a lowering of its profits and even a temporary lack of profits in a general slump, but if the automatism of the labour process breaks down, the very basis of the production relations of capitalism is in jeopardy. The capitalist control over the labour process of production can only operate to the degree to which the postulate of automatism functions. The stages in the development of capitalism can be seen as so many steps in the pursuit of that postulate, and it is from this angle that we can understand the historical necessity of modern science as well as the peculiarity of its logical and methodological formation. As pointed out earlier in this study, the mathematical and experimental method of science established by Galileo secured the possibility of a knowledge of nature from sources other than manual labour. This is the cardinal characteristic of modern science. With a technology dependent on the knowledge of the workers the capitalist mode of production would be an impossibility. Needless to say, however, the self-acting property of the labour process presents itself from the point of view of the capitalist; from that of the workers it looks different indeed!

It is thus not science but ideology in the sense of one-sided class consciousness when, in the seventeenth century, philosophers like Descartes and Hobbes looked upon the outer world as a whole and in all its parts, organic no less than inorganic, as self-operating mechanisms. Marx considers the mechanistic mode of thinking as characteristic of capitalism in the epoch of manufacture. Indeed, so long as this functional self-activity of the labour process had not yet materialised in the technology of machinery it reigned in the mind of the capitalist class, only to lose its imaginative grip when the postulate gains palpable mechanical reality.

However, if the postulate of the self-operating production process had remained nothing more real than an ideology, not far removed from the dream of perpetual motion, the capitalist mode of production could not have materialised. The postulate had to be given reality, and to achieve this was the business of modern science.

19

Galilean Science and the Dynamic Concept of Inertia

The break with tradition resulting in the foundation of exact science occurred when Galileo extended the concept of inertia to movement and thereby initiated the science of dynamics. Until then inertia had always been understood as rest, and rest only, so that movement had required an effort or *impetus* to bring it about or to sustain it. This effort did not reside in things but had to be supplied in the last resort by a human being, handicraftsman or peasant, independent producer or slave or serf or wage-labourer; and even when the movement occurred in nature outside the human range the effort imagined to be causing it was of material forces acting as if with an agency analogous to that of man.

These assumptions of a static inertia and of the need of an impetus to account for movement are in keeping with a handicraft mode of production. Their rational use is limited to the solving of tasks lying within the scope of human strength and skill. They become irrational and fail when applied to problems transcending this scope by a substantial margin, as was notably the case with the ballistics of gunnery which in turn governed the entire range of military engineering and architecture when Europe was gripped by the fear of the Turkish menace (from the fall of Constantinople 1453 and of Otranto 1490).

The calculation of the trajectory of cannon balls was among the foremost problems on which Galileo brought to bear his concept of inertial movement and which he was the first to solve successfully. He proved it to be an exercise of pure mathematical analysis consisting of the combination of two geometrical principles, that of a straight line with a horizontal or an upward tilt and that of a vertical fall involving an even acceleration of known arithmetical measure. The combination yielded a parabola and the actual trajectory of cannon balls proved experimentally to conform with this rule advanced by way of hypothesis, while making allowance for air resistance. We know that Newton later repeated on an astronomical scale in his calculation of celestial orbits the feat which Galileo performed in terrestrial mechanics.

The Galilean assumption of inertial motion opened the applicability of mathematics to the calculation of natural phenomena of motion. This calculation carries scientific reliability, providing that the phenomena can be isolated from uncontrolled environmental influences and then tested experimentally. This briefly epitomises the guiding features of the mathematical and experimental method of science which, in turn, signifies the epistemologically most telling part of the Scientific Revolution associated with the name of Galileo. Our aim in this study is to show that the rise of modern science is not only outwardly coincident but inherently connected with the rise of modern capitalism. In order to do that we must give a historical-materialist account of the origin and inner possibility of the method of modern science.

For a fuller description of the salient characteristics of this method I draw on Alexandre Koyré, whom I regard as one of the most distinguished exponents of the history of science as an internal history of ideas. His is an idealistic witness, but one which I intend to turn to advantage as an added test of the materialistic interpretations here proposed. I quote from his essay on 'Galileo and the Scientific Revolution of the Seventeenth Century', which is a good summary of his extensive Galilean investigations.[32]

> Modern physics, which is born with and in the works of Galileo, looks upon the law of inertial motion as its basic and fundamental law. . . . The principle of inertial motion is very simple. It states that a body, left to itself, remains in a state of motion so long as it is not interfered with by some external force. In other words, a body at rest will remain eternally at rest unless it is 'put in motion', and a body in motion will continue to move, and to persist, in its rectilinear motion and given speed, so long as nothing prevents it from doing so.

It is true that Galileo did not formulate this definition himself, although in his scientific work in terrestrial mechanics and physics he put it into practical effect. His research did not extend to astronomy, and his interest in the controversy around the Copernican system was in the main ideological. In the *Discorsi* of 1638,[33] the last of his dialogues on these issues, he touches upon inertial motion and describes it, by way of illustration, as the movement of a body persisting in a continuous course of uniform speed running parallel to the earth's surface. Thereby he creates the confusing impression that he conceived inertial motion as circular, and, even more misleading, as a notion gleaned from observation and therefore of empirical status. And yet, nothing could be further from the truth. Inertial motion such as Galileo applies in his research is in empty space and strictly rectilinear, which makes it unmistakably non-empirical. Space, empty of air, is no object of perception in the terrestrial sphere, and in outer space, where we may claim to see it, none of the observable phenomena moves in rectilinear but all in orbital fashion.

The immediate successors to Galileo, Descartes and Torricelli, are quite clear on the non-empirical character of Galileo's novel dynamic principle. Newton gave it the final acknowledgement under the name of 'the first law of motion'. There is thus no possible doubt that Galileo's own description in the *Discorsi* must be discounted and that the correct interpretation is the non-empirical one of 'the uniform motion in a right line' – to use Newton's phrasing. Koyré is well justified in emphasising this true aspect of the principle which does not always receive its due attention.

'The principle of inertial motion', he continues where we quoted him before, 'appears to us perfectly clear, plausible, and even, practically, self-evident. . . . The Galilean concept of motion (as well as that of space) seems to us so "natural" that we even believe to have derived it from experience and observation, though, obviously, nobody has ever encountered an inertial motion for the simple reason that such a motion is utterly and absolutely impossible. We are equally well accustomed to the mathematical approach to nature, so well that we are not aware of the boldness of Galileo's statement that "the book of nature is written in geometrical characters", any more than we are conscious of the paradoxical daring of his decision to treat mechanics as mathematics, that is to substitute for the real, experienced world a world of geometry made real, and to explain the real by the impossible.

'In modern science motion is considered as purely geometrical translation from one point to another. Motion, therefore, in no way affects the body which is endowed with it; to be in motion or to be at rest does not make any difference to, or produce a change in, the body in motion or at rest. The body as such is utterly indifferent to both. Consequently, we are unable to ascribe motion to a determined body considered in itself. A body is only in motion in its relation to some other body, which we assume to be at rest. We can therefore ascribe it to the one or to the other of the two bodies, *ad lib*. All motion is relative. Just as it does not affect the body which is endowed with it, the motion of a body in no way interferes with other movements that it may execute at the same time. Thus a body may be endowed with any number of motions which combine to produce a result according to purely geometrical rules, and vice versa, every given motion can be decomposed, according to the same rules, into a number of component ones. . . .

'Thus, to appear evident, the principle of inertial motion presupposes (*a*) the possibility of isolating a given body from all its physical environment, (*b*) the conception of space which identifies it with the homogeneous infinite space of Euclidean geometry, and (*c*) a conception of movement – and of rest – which considers them as states and places them on the same ontological level of being.'[34]

With his usual brevity Bertrand Russell summarises:

Galileo introduced the two principles that did most to make mathematical physics possible: The law of inertial motion, and the parallelogram law.[35]

The vital importance of the principle of inertial motion is that it has the element of motion in common with innumerable phenomena of nature and at the same time it is co-extensive with mathematics and can be treated like Euclidean geometry 'made real', as Koyré puts it. It thus opens the door through which mathematics can establish itself as an instrument of the analysis of given phenomena of movement and yield a mathematical hypothesis which can then be tested experimentally. The concept of inertial motion is the methodological key to exact science. The crucial question is – from what origin does it spring?

We face the contradiction that concepts which are incontestably non-empirical – that is, not gleaned or reflected from nature – can nevertheless give such invaluable service in the investigation of nature. Whether or not the knowledge achieved is proved valid by experiment or by industrial or social practice is, of course, the vital question. But our concern is the possibility of such knowledge which, in order to be available for practical confirmation or refutation, depends on whether the concepts bear the necessary reference to nature at all. And how such reference is possible of concepts which are not taken from nature is the pivot of our enquiry. It can, without exaggeration, be called the particular epistemological riddle of exact science. It was asked by Kant as an enquiry into 'the possibility of pure mathematics and of pure science'. He saw no possible answer other than the one given in his 'transcendental idealism', that, since our knowledge depends on concepts *a priori* not depicting nature as it really is, we can only understand nature as it corresponds to those concepts of ours. In Part I of the present book we have, however, laid the foundation for a different answer, a materialistic one, while changing Kant's ahistorical question to the historical one, to read: How is knowledge of nature possible from sources other than manual labour? or: How is mathematical physics possible given the fact that it cannot be derived from manual labour? How does man acquire an intellectual capacity of knowledge of nature that far exceeds the standards accessible to handicrafts?

Our explanation of the principle of inertial motion is that it derives from the pattern of motion contained in the real abstraction of commodity exchange. This motion has the reality in time and space of the commodity movements in the market, and thus of the circulation of money and of capital. The pattern is absolutely abstract, in the sense of bearing no shred of perceptible qualities, and was defined as: abstract linear movement through abstract, empty, continuous and homogeneous space and time of abstract substances which thereby suffer no material change, the movement being amenable to no other than mathematical treatment. Although continually occurring in our economic life the movement in this description is not perceivable to our private minds. When it does indeed strike our minds it is in a pure conceptual form whose source is no longer recognisable; nor is the mechanism to which it owes its abstractness.

The derivation of Galileo's principle of inertia from the exchange abstraction thus explains the reference of the principle to natural movement. Moreover, it has to be borne in mind that 'the concepts which result from the identification of the elements (the elements of the exchange abstraction) are in origin concepts of nature'.[36] It is necessary to affirm these points in order to counter the impression which might easily arise to a superficial observer that, by tracing the categories of science to a root in social history, we had simply replaced Kant's subjective idealism by a sociological idealism and added historical relativism into the bargain. I recognise that this misapprehension constitutes a danger, because in order to avoid it, an effort must be made to plumb the depth of an argument laden with considerable epistemological complexity.

To bring the right idea to bear on my theory it is advisable to turn to the Afterword to the second German edition of *Capital* where Marx quotes with approval a Russian review of his book and in particular of its method:

> Marx treats the social movement as a process of natural history, governed by laws not only independent of human will, consciousness and intelligence, but rather, on the contrary, determining that will, consciousness, intelligence. (p. 27)

And in the Preface of the first edition Marx speaks of

> My standpoint, from which the evolution of the economic formation of society is viewed as a process of natural history . . . (p. 21)

Thus my derivation of the concepts *a priori* of science is a natural one, not relating, it is true, to the external nature but to the historical nature of man himself.

We must now explain the different concepts of inertia – static in the ages of pure commercial and slave-holding capital in antiquity, and in the Middle Ages and the Renaissance, but dynamic from the start of capitalist production. The first remains as long as the exchange processes are confined to the sphere of circulation as is the case of merchant and monetary capital until the sixteenth century. But as society enters upon a state where the direct producers are without their own means of production then these means of production, both material and men, are brought together by way of the market. Then production does not take place merely as production but as exchange, and exchange no longer signifies only exchange but production. This mingled unity of exchange and production, production and exchange, constitutes a constant and continuous process functioning as an

economically self-compelling system. Production here is of larger
volume and

> Capitalist production only really begins . . . when each in-
> dividual capitalist employs simultaneously a comparatively
> large number of workers, and when, as a result, the labour-
> process is carried on on an extensive scale and yields relatively
> large quantities of products. . . . [This] constitutes the starting
> point of capitalist production. This is true both historically and
> conceptually.[37]

In other words capital is a social power which takes over
production where it has outgrown the economic and technological capacities of the direct producer controlling it himself. While
in the economic field the social power is capital, in the field of
technology it is science, or, more accurately, the methodical
operation of the human mind in its socialised form, guided by its
specific logic, which is mathematics. This socialised mind of man,
we have seen, is money without its material attachments,
therefore immaterial and no longer recognisable as money and,
indeed no longer being money but the 'pure intellect'. In its form
as money it is capital ruling the labour process by the identity of
labour with value and postulating the process to be cast in a
framework in which it operates in an automatic manner
enforcing the embodiment of the labour employed into values
containing a surplus. In its form as the scientific intellect the
socialised mind applies itself to physical phenomena on which the
automatic working of the labour process of the various capitals is
found to be depending. I turn once more to Bertrand Russell's
Human Knowledge[38] to illustrate this context. The first sentence of
the book reads:

> Scientific knowledge aims at being wholly impersonal, and
> tries to state what has been discovered by the collective
> intellect of mankind. (p. 17)

On page 30 we find the statement:

> This principle [of inertial motion] led to the possibility of
> regarding the physical world as a causally self-contained
> system.

The establishment of natural laws we can understand as resulting from a combination of mathematical hypotheses and experiments. How this is helped by, and indeed founded on, the principle of inertial motion, or, let us say, how this was done in classical physics can be further clarified by considering the following statements, one by Engels, the other by Bertrand Russell: In *Anti-Dühring* we read:

> Motion is the mode of existence of matter. Never anywhere has there been matter without motion, nor can there be. Motion in cosmic space, mechanical motion of smaller masses on the various celestial bodies, the motion of molecules as heat or electrical magnetic current, chemical combination or disintegration, organic life – at each given moment each individual atom of matter in the world is in one or other of these forms of motion, or in several forms of them at once.[39]

And in his *History of Western Philosophy* Russell states:

> The theory that the physical world consists only of matter in motion was the basis of the accepted theories of sound, heat, light, and electricity.[40]

The association of matter with motion stems from Galileo's definition of inertia. This definition, we have seen, was the finishing touch enabling Galileo to work out the mathematical and experimental method and to become the founder of modern science. In the light of Galileo's definition of inertia the pattern of the exchange abstraction assumes the meaning of the absolute minimum of what constitutes a physical event. Any event that can be constructed as a composite of this minimum is therefore *ipso facto* conceivable in terms of pure theoretical categories and amenable to full mathematical treatment. This is, in fact, how modern science proceeds. Theoretical hypotheses in conceptual form and mathematical formulation are worked out and tested by confrontation with nature or with that carefully isolated part of nature of which the hypothesis contains the definition. This confrontation represents the experiment. The experiment is carried through with the help of instruments adapted to the hypothesis and are, in fact, part of it. The phenomenon tested is safeguarded from any touch by human hand and made to register specific measurements which are then read as indicated by the instruments, and which must be in answer to the questions advanced by the hypothesis. The act of reading these values is the only direct contact the experimenter is allowed with the piece of nature under investigation. These precautions are indispensable for ascertaining the identity of the tested phenomenon with the mathematical hypothesis; in other words indispensable for clinching the experimental isolation. Owing to this isolation a phenomenon can be subject to investigation only torn out of the context within which it occurs. It is clear, therefore, that modern science is not aimed at helping society in her relations with nature. It studies nature only from the viewpoint of capitalist production. If the experiments yield a reliable verification of the hypothesis the latter becomes an established 'law of nature' in the shape of a law of recurrent events. And this is the result the capitalist may utilise for technological application in his factory. Not infrequently the technological installation closely resembles a large-scale replica of the successful experiment. It can be said that objects over which capital can exercise control must be cast in the form of a commodity. It is the exact truth of exact science that it is knowledge of nature in commodity form.

20

Bourgeois Science

Is it correct to class science as we know it, or rather as we knew it until the end of the nineteenth century, as bourgeois science? Can we expect a major transformation of science if socialism were to supersede capitalism? It all depends what we understand by 'science'. The science that we have is a product of intellectual labour divided from manual labour. For that reason alone it cannot represent our possession of nature, our true relation to nature. By adhering to a concept of science which keeps to this intellectual one-sidedness we should not judge it capable of essential alterations, for instance, major alterations in method and in the use of mathematics. In his Parisian *Economic and Philosophical Manuscripts of 1844* Marx is more outspoken than in his later work about his demands on science and there are two passages which I shall quote. The one has regard of the notion of 'labour' which we ought to keep in mind, the other shows us what conception of 'science' animated Marx's ideas.

The outstanding thing in Hegel's *Phenomenology* and its final outcome – that is, the dialectic of negativity as the moving and generating principle – is (thus) first that Hegel conceives the self-genesis of man as a process . . .; that he grasps the essence of *labour* and comprehends objective man – true, because real man – as the outcome of man's *own labour*. The *real* active orientation of man to himself as a species being (i.e. as a human being),* is only possible by his really bringing out of himself all the *powers* that are his as the *species* man – something which is only possible through the totality of man's actions, as the result of history – is only possible by man's treating these generic powers as objects: and this, to begin with, is again only possible in the form of estrangement.[41]

It is clear that 'labour', here, to Marx means the comprehensive unity of man's mental and physical powers and that only when this unity is achieved can man possibly assume control of his destiny and become master of his social history and his relationship to nature. When we distinguished 'societies of production' and 'societies of appropriation' we made the point that on the basis of primitive communal modes of production, as they preceded commodity production, the social practice was rational but the theory was irrational (mythological and anthropomorphic), while on the basis of commodity production the relation was reversed; namely, the social practice has turned irrational (out of man's control) but his mode of thinking has assumed

---

* Marx later replaces this anthropological Feuerbachian notion of 'species being' (Gattungswesen) with that of the social being and social essence of man.

rational forms. What Marx has in his mind's eye in the passage
we quoted is man's historical potentiality of achieving a rational
practice and a rational theory combined, which is simply another
way of speaking of communism. In the following passage we find
Marx evolving a conception of 'science' corresponding to this
complete rationality of man, the only real one that can be
intended.

It will be seen how the history of industry and the established
objective existence of industry are the *open book of man's essential*
powers, the exposure of the senses of human *psychology*.
Hitherto this was not conceived in its inseparable connection
with man's *essential being*, but only in an external relation of
utility. . . .

A *psychology* for which this, the part of history most
contemporary and accessible to sense, remains a closed book,
cannot become a genuine, comprehensive and *real* science.
What indeed are we to think of a science which *airily* abstracts
from this large part of human labour and which fails to feel its
own incompleteness. . . . [Marx is thinking here chiefly of the
humanities and in the idealistic and romantic manner of his
time of writing – S.-R.]

The *natural sciences* have developed an enormous activity and
have accumulated a constantly growing mass of material.
Philosophy, however, has remained just as alien to them as
they remain to philosophy. Their momentary unity [in Hegel's
Encyclopedia presumably – S.-R.] was only a *chimerical illusion*.
The will was there, but the means was lacking. Even
historiography lays regard to natural science only
occasionally. . . . But natural science has invaded and transformed human life all the more *practically* through the medium
of industry; and has prepared human emancipation, however
directly and much it had to consummate dehumanisation.
Industry is the *actual*, historical relation of nature, and therefore
of natural science, to man. . . . In consequence, natural
science will lose its abstractly material – or rather, its
idealistic – tendency,[42] and will become the basis of *human*
science, as it has already become the basis of actual human life,
albeit in an estranged form. . . . All History is the preparation
for '*man*' to become the object of *sensuous* consciousness, and for

the needs of 'man as man' to become his needs. History itself is a *real* part of *natural history* – of nature's coming to be man. Natural science will in time subsume under itself the science of man, just as the science of man will subsume under itself natural science: there will be *one* science.[43]

Needless to say this is no longer a conception of science which fits the one-sided intellectual science which we have today and which stands out as bourgeois science when confronted with Marx's conception. However, there are signs that our twentieth-century science which has achieved the enormous advance to atomic and nuclear physics has left bourgeois science behind and has assumed a state where it no longer fits the 'rationality' on which capitalism relies for its continuance. In any case, if it possesses the same and even a higher degree of rationality, it does not occupy the place in our present-day capitalist society which nineteenth-century science held, for it has unleashed natural powers which capital fails to control. Thus if we remain in the clutches of capitalism we are threatened with the loss of the social rationality of science which capitalism formerly possessed and may find ourselves with the irrationality of our social practice combined with no less an irrationality of our theory. If we are not mistaken, man has reached a crossroad where he is faced with the alternative either of taking the socialist road and perhaps achieving a rationality of both social practice and theory or continuing on the capitalist road and forfeiting both.

PART III

THE DUAL ECONOMICS OF ADVANCED CAPITALISM

2 1

From De-socialised to Re-socialised Labour

In Part I of this book we have argued that intellectual labour divided from manual labour is ruled by a logic of appropriation. Socialism, however, demands a mode of thinking in accordance with a logic of production. This implies thinking by the direct producers themselves and it would necessitate the unity of head and hand.

It is our purpose now to investigate trends which dominate our present epoch with regard to this contrast. The reasoning involved is, of course, grounded in what has been set out in the preceding chapters. It is bound, however, to be a great deal more speculative since it is concerned with the present and future, and serves, it is hoped, as a basis for further research by others.

We have seen that the abstract intellectual work associated with the system of commodity production is an *a priori* 'socialised' form of thinking, in antithesis to physical labour 'carried on independently and privately by individual producers'[1] since 'only products of mutually independent acts of labour, performed in isolation, can confront each other as commodities'.[2] The abstract intellect arose because labour lost its primitive collective form of working and became de-socialised in such a way that the cohesion of society grew dependent on exchange instead of production. As the vehicle of the social synthesis, or of societisation, as we might call it, exchange becomes monetary exchange activated by money being utilised as capital. In the initial epochs of commodity exchange capital figured in the 'antediluvian form', as Marx called it, of monetary and merchant capital, only since then to seize upon the means of production and to operate them by wage-labour.

The logic of appropriation cannot be expected to change into a logic of production so long as labour has not resumed its capacity of carrying the social synthesis. The antithesis between intellectual and physical labour will not vanish before the private and fragmented labour of commodity production has been turned into re-socialised labour. But, as we know only too well, this in itself will not be enough. The re-socialised labour must become the societising force which must bring about the unity of head and hand that will implement a classless society.

22

A Third Stage of the Capitalist Mode of Production?

In the era of flow-production the socialisation of labour has reached a stage higher than ever before, but of course in subordination to capital. The re-socialisation of labour has been a major trend, if not indeed the main one, in capitalist history. Marx distinguishes two stages of the process: the stage of manufacture followed by that of machinery and large-scale industry – 'machinofacture' in short. We feel there may be good reasons for distinguishing a third stage. As Marx says:

> In manufacture the transformation of the mode of production takes labour-power as its starting-point. In large-scale industry, on the other hand, the instruments of labour are the starting-point.[3]

In monopoly capitalism and its flow methods of production, I would continue, it is labour itself that forms the starting-point. The ground for distinguishing this third stage lies in major structural changes in the labour process occurring in pursuit of intensified valorisation of capital. But the postulate of the automatism of the labour process innate in capital, and its increasing realisation, merits our attention.

In the epoch of manufacture, representing the initial stage of the capitalist mode of production, capital employs the existing artisans of the pre-capitalist period as wage labourers and fits them into a closely knit system of division of labour. Working under extreme pressure of time, a marked increase of labour productivity of each worker is guaranteed, with a correspondingly greater amount of surplus labour to capital. These artisans are transformed from a mass of individual workers doing various jobs in handicraft workshops into an organised collective or compound worker (Gesamtarbeiter) though still only using handtools.

> The collective worker, who constitutes the living mechanism of manufacture, is made up solely of such one-sidedly specialised workers [who each] performs the same simple operation for the whole of his life [and thereby] converts his body into the automatic, one-sided implement of that operation.[4]

But, as we have quoted before:

> since handicraft skill is the foundation of manufacture, and since the mechanism of manufacture as a whole possesses no objective framework which would be independent of the workers themselves, capital is constantly compelled to wrestle with the insubordination of the workers.[5]

In fact the automatism of the labour process upon which capital depends for its control over production is not vested in the human labourer but in conditions which determine the quantity of his expenditure of the labour-power he has sold to the capitalist. The capitalist does not enforce his will by his direct personal action but only indirectly by the action of things and services which he can buy with his money and watch over with his authority.

The answer to the unsolved problem of manufacture was of course the introduction of machinery into the labour process. Of the three parts of the machinery which Marx distinguishes – 'the motor mechanism, the transmitting mechanism and the tool or working machine' – 'it is this last part of the machinery with which the industrial revolution began'.[6] For this part of the machinery 'replaces the worker, who handles a single tool, by a mechanism operating with a number of similar tools and set in motion by a single motive power . . .'.[7]

Indeed the exposition of Marx in the opening of the fifteenth chapter is so well known that it might seem redundant to quote further here. However, before arguing my case for distinguishing a third stage of capitalist development I want to throw into relief the very features of Marx's exposition which seem to leave no room for such a stage, because he includes in his second stage the most advanced characteristics of the modern labour process, including the continuous flow method and the automatic character of present-day production.

> The collective working machine, which is now an articulated system composed of various kinds of single machine, and of groups of single machines, becomes all the more perfect the more the process as a whole becomes a continuous one, i.e. the less the raw material is interrupted in its passage from the first phase to the last; in other words, the more its passage from one phase to another is effected not by the hand of man, but by the machinery itself. . . . As soon as a machine system executes, without man's help, all the movements required to elaborate the raw material, and needs only supplementary assistance from the worker, we have an automatic system of machinery, capable of constant improvement in its details. . . . An organised system of machines to which motion is communicated by the transmitting mechanism from an automatic centre is the most developed form of production by machinery.[8]

The description given here might stretch to the forms of production of the twentieth century right to the present day. To what extent this is the case is shown by the following quotations from *Grundrisse*:

From the moment . . . when fixed capital has developed to a certain extent – and this extent, as we indicated, is the measure of the development of large industry generally – . . . from this instant on, every interruption of the production process acts as a direct reduction of capital itself, of its initial value. . . . Hence, the greater the scale on which fixed capital develops . . . the more does the continuity of *the production process* or the constant flow of reproduction become an externally compelling condition for the mode of production founded on capital.[9]

and again:

Hence the *continuity* of production becomes an external necessity for capital with the development of that portion of it which is determined as fixed capital. For circulating capital, an interruption . . . is only an interruption in the creation of surplus value. But with fixed capital, the interruption . . . is the destruction of its original value itself. Hence the continuity of the production process which corresponds to the concept of capital is posited as *conditio sine qua* for its maintenance only with the development of fixed capital.[10]

It seems difficult to find room for a third stage of the capitalist mode of production after reading these passages. But what they do not show are the implications carried by the external necessity of the continuity of the production process. These implications cover the evolution of monopoly capitalism, scientific management and flow production.

23

The Turn to
Monopoly Capitalism

In line with Lenin we consider these developments as distinctive characteristics of a new stage of the capitalist mode of production. Lenin related the change to the level of the organic composition of capital or the high grade of capital intensity reached in the last quarter of the nineteenth century (in the heavy industries of iron and steel manufacture, synthetic chemistry and electro-industry). This is, in fact, synonymous with the terminology of Marx in *Grundrisse*, which Lenin, of course, did not know. But his theoretical reasoning has been refined and substantiated by certain non-Marxist studies bearing on the same subject. The most pertinent ones are *Studies in the Economics of Overhead Cost* by J. M. Clark[11] and the works by Eugen Schmalenbach, the founder and most important representative of modern management sciences in Germany.[12]

The reasoning is simple and incontrovertible. Growing capital intensity and a rising organic composition of capital leads, at a certain point, to a changing costing structure of production, amounting to an increasing dominance of the so-called indirect or fixed element of the cost. This does not vary with output and still remains constant even when production, as in a severe slump, might have to stop temporarily altogether. These invariable overheads are made up of the interest on loaned capital, depreciation, insurance, maintenance, leases, rents and so on. Firms wherein this part of the cost is high in relation to the direct costs, in the main of materials and wages which vary according to the volume of output, cannot easily respond to the market regulatives of social economy controlling the play of the law of value. When demand recedes and prices tend to slump, production should be cut down and supplies be diminished. But heavy overheads will cause unit costs to rise with lessened output, and we obtain the contradiction that adaptation of supplies to receding demands forces the cost to rise when prices fall. In other words the rising organic composition of capital makes production increasingly inadaptable to the market regulatives. The reaction to this contradiction on the part of the firms affected can only be to force them, as a matter of life and death, to try to obtain control of the movements of the market. This is how they become 'monopolists'.

Under the impact of this causality some of the features of the labour process described by Marx assume a changed significance.

24

Imperialism and Scientific Management

These conditions occurred increasingly and over a spreading range of industry during the last quarter of the nineteenth century. They assumed a spectacular manifestation in the long depression following upon the slump of 1873/4 and lasting almost uninterruptedly for more than twenty years. The period, remembered as 'the hungry eighties', was a time of mass unemployment comparable to that of the 1930s; a time of hunger marches and mass demonstrations, of strikes and riots and revolutionary class struggle. Socialism for the first time became the catchword of broad political movements resulting in the founding of social mass parties matched by the organisation of the semi-skilled and even the unskilled workers in a new type of trade unionism. The most ominous features of the picture drawn by

Marx of the impending 'expropriation of the expropriators' seemed to menace the bourgeois world.

Foremost in the picture was the paralysing decline of the rate of profit, the root cause of all the trouble as predicted by Marx. It was felt most acutely in the industries with the highest organic composition of capital, the heavy iron and steel manufacture, synthetic chemistry and electro-industry. The period was particularly prolific in technological and organisational innovations attempting to overcome the paralysing overheads but in fact only aggravating the underlying contradiction so long as the market exercised its unhampered rule. Several initiatives were undertaken towards 'regulating production and thereby also prices and profits', as Engels mentions in a well-known footnote in the third volume of *Capital*.[13] They were effective in producing two hectic booms each of which, however, collapsed within a year. For until the early nineties, the time of Engels's writing, what he adds was still true: that 'these experiments are bound to break down under the pressure of a new economic downturn'. But only a very few years later his remarks ceased to hold true, and it is correct to state that capitalism entered the long depression of the 1870s in the position of a free-market economy and emerged from it in 1895/6 in the shape of consolidated monopoly capitalism.

Two things were above all imperative for the survival of capitalism at that juncture: the first, an expansion of the markets by opening up new territories and resuming colonial expansion on a new scale, a way recommending itself easiest to the rich European creditor countries like Britain, France, Belgium and Holland; the second, a substantial increase in the rate of exploitation of the labour employed in the industries at home, a particular need for the United States, still a debtor country, but rapidly advancing in industry and with the world's highest wage level. In the subsequent course of events both these remedies in conjunction proved necessary to keep capitalism afloat, especially after the First World War when the U.S.A. had turned into the dominant capitalist creditor power. The weakened European countries then followed suit, but with varying time-lags and as reluctant modernisers – with one exception: Germany. Through her defeat and territorial retrenchment as well as loss of foreign capital, Germany had been thrown into the anomalous position of a highly industrialised debtor country.

This left her little choice but to enhance the exploitation of her own labour force by industrial 'rationalisation' on the lines heralded by the American drive for 'scientific managment'.

To underline the parallelism of the two lines of development by which capitalism wrenched itself out of the paralysing fetters of the outmoded free-market system and on to the open-ceiling economics of monopoly capitalism, it suffices to repeat from Lenin's 'Imperialism'[14] the conversation he quotes of Cecil Rhodes with *The Times* correspondent Wickham Steed in 1895:

I was in the East End of London yesterday and attended a meeting of the unemployed. I listened to the wild speeches, which were just a cry for 'bread, bread, bread', and on my way home I pondered over the scene and I became more than ever convinced of the importance of imperialism. . . . My cherished idea is a solution for the social problem, i.e. in order to save the 40,000,000 inhabitants of the United Kingdom from a bloody civil war, we colonial statesmen must acquire new lands for settling the surplus population, to provide new markets for the goods produced in the factories and mines. The Empire, as I have always said, is a bread and butter question. If you want to avoid civil war you must become imperialists.

The year 1895 was also that in which Frederick Winslow Taylor introduced his work to the American Society of Mechanical Engineers with a lecture to which he gave the remarkable title *A Piece Rate System, being a step toward a Partial Solution of the Labor Problem.*[15]

25

The Economy of Time and 'Scientific Management'

The dominance of overhead cost is associated with a specific economy of time relating to the labour process of production. The more highly the production capacity of a given plant is utilised, that is to say, the more products are turned out in a given time and, as a consequence, the quicker the capital can be turned over, then the lower is the unit cost of the output and the greater the competitiveness of the enterprise. The speed of operations in utilising the given plant of a firm is the all-important factor in the competitive struggle for profit under conditions of monopoly capitalism.

If we look back to the beginnings of the search for modern so-called scientific management we can see that it was this economy of time which spurred it on. Harry Braverman points to the vital interconnection:

> It will already have been noticed that the crucial developments in the process of production date from precisely the same period as monopoly capitalism. Scientific management and the whole 'movement' for the organisation of production on its modern basis have their beginnings in the last two decades of the last century. And the scientific technical revolution, based on the systematic use of science for the more rapid transformation of labor power into capital, also begins . . . at the same time. . . . Both chronologically and functionally, they are part of the new stage of capitalist development, and they grow out of monopoly capitalism and make it possible.[16]

I would say that they grew out of the root cause which gave rise to monopoly capitalism, the dominance of overhead cost, i.e. the rise in the organic composition of capital. And coupled with the speeding of operations was the question of its control.

From the lecture by F. W. Taylor already mentioned there ensued a discussion with H. R. Towne and F. A. Halsey, his main rivals, who had put their 'Premium Plan' of management before the same Society in 1891. The central issue of the debate concerns the question of control. In the Towne – Halsey plan[17] 'the control of the speed problem is turned over to the men', whereas according to Taylor's scheme it 'lies with the management'. And the main reasoning involved is one of the economics of overhead cost. Indirect expenses equal or exceed the wages paid directly and remain approximately constant whether the output is great or small. Greater output justifies higher wages, the diminution of the indirect portion of the cost per piece being greater than the increase in wages.

The operating economic factor is the effect that the volume of output has on the unit cost. Or, as Taylor later puts it in his *Principles of Scientific Management* (1911)[18] 'it pays the employer to pay higher wages as long as the higher output does not increase overheads'. And there is no doubt that Taylor grasped the implications of this economics of time with greater systematic consistency from the standpoint of monopoly capital than anybody else among the would-be founders of the appropriate sort of management at that time. Taylor was the one to whom the claim to be its founder rightfully belongs. Let us go through some of the salient points of his system.

26

The Essentials of Taylorism

Frederick Winslow Taylor's first writing was the lecture of 1895 given to the American Society of Mechanical Engineers, from which we have already quoted: *A Piece Rate System, being a step towards a Partial Solution of the Labor Problem*. This was the first public intimation of his major work of which the final publication did not appear until 1906 under the title of *On the Art of Cutting Metals*, a very meticulous book indeed, divided into 1198 paragraphs and supplemented by twenty-four folders of charts. It has fallen into undeserved oblivion and much better known are the two more popular books *Shop Management* (1903) and *Principles of Scientific Management* (1911).[19]

The cornerstone of scientific management is the time-and-motion study of operations. Of this Taylor says: 'What the writer wishes particularly to emphasize is that this whole system rests upon the accurate and scientific study of unit times which is by far the most important element in scientific management.' (*Shop Management*.) In its original conception, inspired by his un-disguised concern for the rate of labour exploitation, Taylorism aroused the opposition and revulsion of the workers to an extent which threatened to defeat its own objectives, and therefore it has since been modified and wrapped around with a medley of 'sciences' – physiology, psychology, sociology and so on. But nothing can conceal the hard core of Taylorism which is in force today as it ever was, though the technicalities may have altered.

His principles are expounded in the following extracts from *On the Art of Cutting Metals*.

In the fall of 1880, the machinists in the small machine shop of the Midvale Steel Company, Philadelphia, most of whom were working on piecework in machining locomotive tires, car axles, and miscellaneous forgings, had combined to do only a certain number of pieces per day on each type of work. The writer, who was the newly appointed foreman of the shop, realised that it was possible for the men to do in all cases much more work per day than they were accomplishing. He found, however, that his efforts to get the men to increase their output were blocked by the fact that his knowledge of just what combination of depth of cut, feed, and cutting speed would in each case do the work in the shortest time, was much less accurate than that of the machinists who were combined against him. His conviction that the men were not doing half as much as they should do, however, was so strong that he obtained permission of the management to make a series of experiments to investigate the laws of cutting metals with a view to obtaining a knowledge at least equal to that of the combined machinists who were under him. He expected that these experiments would last not longer than six months. [para. 7]

Instead of six months his investigation took him twenty-six years.

A study of the recommendations made throughout this paper will illustrate the fact that we propose to take all the important decisions and planning which vitally affect the output of the shop out of the hands of the workmen, and centralise them in a few men, each of whom is especially trained in the art of making those decisions and in seeing that they are carried out, each man having his own particular function in which he is supreme, and not interfering with the functions of other men. [para. 124]

While his experiments resulted in many valuable discoveries and inventions (e.g. self-hardening steels and new designs of machine-tools)

we regard as by far the greatest value that portion of our experiments and of our mathematical work which has resulted in the development of the slide rules which enable the shop managers, without consulting the workmen to fix a daily task with a definite time allowance for each workman who is running a machine tool, and to pay the men a bonus for rapid work [para. 51]

a slide rule which

serves to make out the effect which each of 12 variables has upon the choice of cutting speed and feed [para. 6]

and again:

The gain from these slide rules is far greater than that of all the other improvements combined, because it accomplishes the

original object for which in 1880 the experiments were started;
i.e., that of taking the control of the machine shop out of the
hands of the many workmen, and placing it completely in the
hands of the management, thus superseding the 'rule of
thumb' by scientific control. [para. 52] Under our system the
workman is told minutely just what he is to do and how he is to
do it; and any improvement which he makes upon the orders
given him is fatal to success. [para. 118]

Towards the end of his paper he emphasises that

he did not under-estimate the difficulties of and resistance to
using the slide rules. He would add, however, that he looks
upon task management as of such great moment, both to the
workmen in raising their wages and rendering strikes and
labour troubles unnecessary and to the manufacturers in
increasing and cheapening output, that he staked the re-
mainder of his days to further assisting in the putting into
practice his conception of management. [para. 1197]

The crucial advantage and novelty he claimed for his system of
management was that it made the rise of profits for the
manufacturer compatible with rising wages for the workers. In
his own words: 'High wages and low labour cost are not only
compatible, but are, in the majority of cases mutually con-
ditional.' (*Shop Management*, pp. 21–2.) This is why he saw in it a
partial solution of the labour problem, and in 1895 he even
expressed the hope that it would contribute to the elimination of
the trade cycle, thus freeing capitalism of its two major evils.
Taylor's examples given in *Shop Management* show increases in
workers' output up to 300 per cent and even 400 per cent relative
to a wage increase of 60 per cent! Inflexibility of the cost structure
being also the main element making for monopolism, it becomes
apparent why Taylorism has its roots in monopoly capitalism.
Nor does the causality stop there. Taylor's personal history serves
to illustrate how Taylorism itself acts on monopolism. After
three or four years' work at the Midvale Steel Company he
transferred his activity to the Bethlehem Steel Company, where
he totally reorganised the system of management; subsequently
the latter forged a merger with the former to found the United

Steel Company, the biggest of its kind in the United States. Thus Taylorism, in its turn, helped to increase the stimulus instigating monopolism.

27

Critique of Taylorism

An explanation is needed for the quotations in the last chapter dealing with Taylor's much advertised slide rules which hardly reached any practical importance after the introduction of transfer mechanisms and the flow-method of production had rendered them redundant. However I quote them for a number of reasons. In the first place the immense time and trouble which Taylor devoted to them explain why he spent twenty-six years on the completion of his main work. Second, they demonstrated Taylor's singleness of purpose in wanting to transfer the whole skill and experience possessed by the craftsmen of metal trades upon the management. This knowledge in the hands of management was transformed into an intellectual feat transcribed into a set of norms and rules. It thereby became a possession of the managers to deal with in the interests of capital; they could carve it up, mechanise the subdivisions and even automate it as a whole. Taylor refers to this knowledge in its original form as 'all the important decisions and planning which vitally affect the output of the shop'.

The third reason why I regard Taylor's work on his slide rules of such importance is the clarity with which it shows that such knowledge, if left in the possession of the craftsman, must be linked inseparably with his manual labour, representing his productive capacity as an individual worker. But it also enshrines everything which makes possible the link-up of co-operating craftsmen into 'one collective worker'. This socialisation of their labour, which should, by rights, constitute the power of the workers in production, if not even over production, is removed from them by the Taylorisation of their labour, which instead gives management the means to wield technological coercion upon the workers.

In paragraph 116 of *On the Art of Cutting Metals* Taylor proclaims 'and but little can be accomplished with these laws' (derived from the slide rules) 'unless the old-style foremen and shop-superintendents have been done away with, and functional foremenship has been substituted – consisting of speed bosses, gang bosses, order-of-work men, inspectors, time-study men etc.' In this type of management created by Taylor are concentrated all the powers needed for ensuring the postulate of automatism necessary for the control of capital over production. Monopoly capitalism does indeed represent a third stage of the capitalist mode of production, the one in which it reaches its acme.

As early as 1903, in *Shop Management,* Taylor stresses that 'time study is a success only if it enables you to know exactly how long the studied job *should* take', and not only how long it *does* take in any given case. And he goes on to say: 'The best way to do this, in fact almost the only way in which the timing can be done with certainty, is to divide the men's work into its elements and time each element separately as "unit times".' It amounts, of course, to nothing more than a mere pretence to proclaim the arbitrarily fixed time rates for a job (in units or no units) as norms of independent validity – as if they were extracted miraculously from the bosom of nature or even represented some prescience of the intellect! But this pretence is common practice in all capitalist countries where 'scientific job analysis' is in use. The pretence is inseparable from the whole intention of Taylorism. Under the German Refa-system, for instance, all kinds of manual operations are broken down into six basic elements of motion, and these are again minutely subdivided until the smallest imaginable common particle of these subdivisions is finally allocated a fractional measure of time counted in hundredths of a second!

It is of the essence of Taylorism that the standards of labour timing are not to be mistaken for the empiricism of the work as the workers themselves do it. Taylor does not learn his time measure from the workers; he imparts the knowledge of it as the laws for their work. The whole claim of 'science' for his functional task management hinges upon the 'accurate and scientific study of time units, the most important element in scientific management'. *Coercive timing* would be an appropriate name to give to this element. It corresponds to the treatment of productive human work in accordance with the logic of appropriation. For if we remind ourselves of the analysis of 'abstract time and space' in Part I, it can be seen how the handing over of a coin in payment for a commodity separates the time of the act from all its contents; thereby time is abstractified to a quantifiable dimension into which the scientific intellect can refit carefully selected items of content to make out the mathematics of their laws of behaviour in nature cast in commodity form. Precisely this kind of thing happens in Taylorism, but now applying to the absolute antipode to the logic of appropriation, namely to active human labour in its very labour process. Here the intellect, acting in the service of the capitalist power of appropriation, can assume the mere pretence of its legitimacy in wielding a fictitious norm of labour timing.

It is small wonder, therefore, that we can recognise in the work of Taylor and his followers a tendency to progress from empirical timing to 'synthetic timing' where the time norm for a job is construed without consulting or watching the worker, even for new jobs which have never yet been practised. The first man hired will find himself faced with his technologistical prerequisites and with the precise time and pay rates for the jew job. The proper methods of synthetic timing were evolved, not by Taylor himself, but soon after his death by his pupil Frank Gilbreth.[20] The principle, although it bears the latter's name, was clearly conceived by Taylor and dates back to 1903 at the very latest. Its present-day application in the systems of the measured day-rate or the MTM presents therefore no departure from Taylorism, but rather its further fulfilment.

In strict keeping with the characteristics of Taylorism is the fact that the concepts of time and motion used in its job analysis are *technological categories* and no true terms of human labour at all. Taylorised labour, therefore, is human labour made into a technological entity, homogeneous with the machinery, directly adaptable and can be inserted or transformed into it without any difficulty of conversion. Here labour is not only subsumed economically to capital (to use Marx's expression), i.e. by the act of the workmen selling their labour-power to the capitalist, but also physically and technologically. This is a difference which at first sight may seem of small portent. In actual fact, however, it represents the basis and starting-point for the process leading up to the automation of human labour in the precise technical sense of the term. To say this does not minimise the importance nor deny the validity of what Marx states of capitalist production in its machine age generally. As we have partly quoted before:

> Every kind of capitalist production, in so far as it is not only a labour process but also capital's process of valorization, has this in common; that it is not the worker who employs the conditions of his work, but rather the reverse, the conditions of work employ the worker. However, it is only with the coming of machinery that this inversion first acquires a technical and palpable reality. Owing to its conversion into an automaton, the instrument of labour confronts the worker during the labour process in the shape of capital, dead labour, which dominates and soaks up living labour-power. The separation of the intellectual faculties of the production process from manual labour, and the transformation of those faculties into powers exercised by capital over labour, is . . . finally completed by large-scale industry erected on the foundation of machinery. The special skill of each individual machine-operator, who has now been deprived of all significance, vanishes as an infinitesimal quantity in the face of the science, the gigantic natural forces, and the mass of social labour embodied in the system of machinery, which, together with those three forces, constitute the power of the 'master'.[21]

This is indeed a far-sighted anticipation of the development of capitalism, foreshadowing even the stages it fully reached only under monopoly capital. The specificities of the third stage, however, such as the wedding together rather than the confrontation of labour and machinery; the conversion of the worker from a machine-operator into a part of the machinery; the new forms and further extension of the division of mental and manual labour to the labour process itself, – these do not find expression in the above passage of Marx. What it does express, however, is that which both the second and third stages have in common. But the existence of common features does not lessen the immense importance of the distinctive characteristics which occur in the monopolistic stage. The direct analysis and normative measurement of labour already discussed is one of these characteristics, to which we shall return later. The division of head and hand connected with it is equally striking and perhaps of greater implication.

In *Shop Management* Taylor states that his system 'is aimed at establishing a clearcut and novel division of mental and manual labour throughout the workshops. It is based upon the precise time and motion study of each workman's job in isolation and relegates the entire mental parts of the tasks in hand to the managerial staff . . . working out minutely detailed job-cards which the workmen are left to follow out in the prescribed speed.'[22] This latter detail was drastically changed when flow methods came to be introduced somewhat later, causing, however, no mitigation but only further accentuation of the schism made by Taylor between the mind and the body of the industrial workman. The workman has, as it were, handed over his mind to a new institution which has come into existence – the modern management in charge of the economy of time peculiar to monopoly capital.

This new division of mental and manual labour must not be confused nor assumed identical with the fundamental one, dating from classical antiquity, now mainly rooted in the intellectual nature of science, although there are of course links and changes in the practice of science which reinforce these links. But the division directly involved in the managerial authority over the monopolistic labour process is the one between the technical and organisational intelligentsia and the manual work-force. As this division springs from the foundations from which monopoly capitalism itself arises, the stability of monopoly capitalism vitally depends on the relations between these two forces, the mental and manual, remaining safely divided. Should the division be changed into an alliance the authority of the management would be in jeopardy. Acting in unison the direct producers could dispose of the capitalist management and take production into their own control.

The cultivation of the specific fetishism of the modern monopolistic management is, therefore, one of the particular ideological concerns, not only of the capitalists themselves, but of the State. The fetishism has a twofold root. The intellectual tasks vested in this management are not seen as representing the workers' mind but as deriving directly or indirectly from science and scientific technology. The mysticism of the 'scientific-technical revolution' is its mainstay. Above and beyond that, science itself is the principal issue of our autonomous intellect. This assumption about the intellect is made almost unassailable by modern positivism which places the origins of science outside the range of questions which can be asked; asking such questions is declared metaphysical and nonsensical. Never has idealism led a more unharassed existence!

The second root of the managerial fetishism rests in the individualism of the worker's wage. We have already quoted the important passage from Marx from his chapter on 'Co-operation' where he shows how the 'productive power developed by the worker socially . . . appears as a power which capital possesses by its nature – a productive power inherent in capital'.[23] This 'crucial inversion' of the productive power of collective labour into the power of capital is magnified in monopoly capitalism because in the size of the modern system the workers are more powerless than they have ever been since slavery, owing to the minuteness of each individual contribution. However, this aspect of monopoly capital can be fully discussed only on the basis of the all-important sequence to Taylorism – flow production, which made its very earliest beginnings by Swift in Chicago[24] and Henry Ford in Detroit two years before Taylor's death.[25] As far as I can see, Taylor's writings themselves contain no intimation of flow methods of production.

28

The Foundation of Flow Production

In keeping with Marxian thinking we have interpreted the increase in labour productivity as occurring concurrently with increased association of labour. But it is clearly not the time-and-motion study as instituted by Taylor which socialises labour. The most striking and best-known examples of Taylor's work, famous from his own writings, refer to operations of building workers and to simple loading tasks in a yard of the Bethlehem Steel Co.; not only were these loading operations done by hand with shovels, but they had been done collectively as gang labour before Taylor individualised them. Indeed, one of the essentials in his instructions on time-and-motion study reads that each analysis must be applied to the operation concerned 'in strict isolation'.[26] This ruling would make it quite immaterial whether the operation studied was done singly or as part of co-ordinated labour. The relevance of Taylorism to highly socialised production is not that the specific norm of labour it imposes either causes the socialisation nor presumes its previous existence. It lies in the fact that Taylorism serves to implement the specific economy of time inherent in monopoly capitalism; and the economy of time ensues from high overhead costs and the need for continuous production.

The classical example best suited for illustrating this relationship is Ford's foundation of his motor works on the basis of flow production from 1913 onwards. In the building up of the operation Taylorism played no part. The stop watch need hardly have been invented, it seems, from the description Henry Ford himself gives in *My Life and Work*. The decisive element was the organisation of mass-production of a uniform product. He left much room for the inventiveness of his workers, and the scheme did not develop at one stroke but evolved piecemeal, always following the logic of continuous mass-production. Ford's idea was to concentrate on one model car, his 'model T', designed by him personally for simplicity of operation, ease of repair, lightness of weight and multiplicity of use. He was the first to anticipate that the market for cars was unlimited, providing that the price could be kept at a lower level than anyone at the time thought possible. Other manufacturers were designing in-dividual cars with a variety of models at high prices aimed at a restricted market for use as a privilege by the rich. Ford's famous remark illustrates his way of thinking. 'Any customer can have a car painted any colour that he wants so long as it is black.'[27] Incidentally he was also the first to realise the value of the uniformity of a product acting as its own advertisement.

In the building up of his production process overhead cost was not a compelling factor. The relation was the reverse: the overheads and their increasing dominance resulted from the flow methods applied in creating this new and revolutionary type of mechanised mass-production. The application of Taylorism became a necessity, apparently even to Ford's personal dislike, but indispensable if he was to maintain his profits and his competitiveness.

Thus it is not sufficient to look from the viewpoint of the engineer only at the history of flow production in capitalism since the industrial revolution and the growth of large-scale industry. True, seen from a purely technological angle no more than a replacement of multi-purpose by single-purpose machine-tools is needed for introducing some measure of flow production. There is no reason why this should not have happened as far back as the beginning of the nineteenth century or still earlier if the product was simple enough and the demand for it sufficiently large and pressing. Emergencies arising from war were the most likely occasions, such as the sudden mass requirements for small arms in the American Civil War. Mass-production on a flow-method basis appeared as the only device which could supply demands quickly. The need for munitions in the First World War created similar conditions on a much larger scale. But does the tech-nological similarity place these instances on the same level with the Ford works of Detroit? The difference should be easy to recognise. The instances prior to the emergence of monopoly capitalism were motivated by reasons of use-value and the urgency of war-time need, whereas twentieth-century flow production follows the logic of exchange-value and the time economy enforced by heavy overheads. Thus the serial small-arms manufacture of the 1860s went out of existence and was forgotten as soon as the Civil War was over, while Henry Ford's initiative introduced a new epoch of the capitalist mode of production.

29

The Unity of Measurement of Man and Machine

The flow method of manufacture is the mode of production most perfectly adapted to the demands of the economy of time in monopoly capital. The entirety of a workshop or factory is integrated into one continuous process in the service of the rule of speed. We remember Marx saying: 'The collective working machine . . . becomes all the more perfect the more the process as a whole becomes a continuous one. . . .'[28] This continuity is now implemented by a machine, a conveyor belt or other transfer mechanism subjecting to the set speed the action of all the productive machinery and the human labour serving it. The identical rhythm of time of the transfer mechanism and the unity of measurement it imposes between the men and machines constitute the distinguishing principle of the flow method of modern mass-production. Compound machinery with com-pound labour works under this unity of measurement. Linked by the action of a transfer mechanism the workers operate like one comprehensive functional labourer using perhaps 400, 800 or

2000 hands and feet of individuals doing minutely fragmented jobs of work. This mechanised form of mass-production is a system in which human labour is coerced into complete technological combination.

Clearly, industrial plants organised on principles of continuous flow must follow their own rules of development. Strict synchronisation of all part-processes is essential. Any section slower than the others acts as a bottleneck condemning the capital invested in the plant to wasteful utilisation. Further capital must be invested until the plant satisfies the rule of even flow. The result will be the growth of the actual volume of output and of the permanent capacity of the plant. This result may or may not be intended nor called for in terms of market demands. If not, the firm stands to lose in the market what it gains by observing the laws of internal plant economy.

Here we notice the gap which opens up, in monopoly capitalism, between market economy and plant economy. For the laws determining the structure and evolution of the production process of monopoly capital are rooted in its intrinsic time economy and relate directly to the labour process of production. But these laws exist, of course, side by side with, and in the framework of, market economy; otherwise the enormous advance in labour productivity and surplus production springing from the new methods would not transmit themselves into private profits.

The unity of measurement of machinery and labour introduces a new setting for the class struggle in the labour process. The unity of measurement can either be one of the subordination of labour to the machinery or it can take the shape of the subordination of the machinery to labour. It must be one of the two; it cannot remain indifferent to this alternative. Under capitalist management, of course, the first is taken for granted, the assumption being that the workers, while working as a combined force with their hands, in their minds remain divided in conformity with their pay-packets. For the contrary case to become possible, the minds of the workers should be set in conformity with the compound character of their combined labour. An example of this rare possibility was shown by the workers at the Pirelli strike in Italy in 1968, when they did their own timing by 'counter-norms' and succeeded in taking the assembly lines out of the hands of the management into their own, and reduced the flow to as low as 30 per cent of the rated speed.

This and many strikes of a similar kind, as well as numerous factory occupations in Italy, France, England and elsewhere, illustrate the fact that the fetishism, observed by Marx, involving the 'inversion' of the relationship between labour and capital has worn thin in a type of production where both labour and machinery assume compound structure.

Capital continuously faces the necessity for restructuring its production process, not only to reduce unit costs and to elude recessions, but even more compellingly to retain its hold over the class struggle. Thus the present drive towards group-work to replace the rigid linear pattern of assembly work may be apparent concessions to the workers, but in fact are nearly always aimed at breaking the bargaining power which the working class have learned to exert from line work. Another response of capital to industrial strife is continuous 'rationalisation' of production by having less and less workers and more and more automation regardless of the long-term perils of this trend.

30

The Dual Economics of Monopoly Capitalism

The system of monopoly capitalism is marked by a duality of economics, the one located in the market and going back to roots as old as commodity production itself, the other peculiar to the most recent form of production and pointing to the latest, if not the last, stage of capitalism. But the rules of the market are no longer the same as in free-market capitalism. In the free-market system production was, as a rule, tied to the manufacture of reproductive values – that is, to values serving the reproduction process of society – and these values were represented by marketable goods. The reproduction of capital thus ran, by and large, parallel to that of society, although submitting it to the wasteful vicissitudes of the trade cycle. By the manipulation of the market characteristic of monopolism this functional tie-up between production and circulation has been increasingly weakened. Monopolistic production is no longer bound to the manufacture of reproductive values, and the consolidation of monopolism in the middle 90s of the last century was marked by the beginning of an arms race leading up to the First World War. Obviously, an ever-growing part of the gross national product consisted of non-marketable goods for which the State devolved the cost upon the shoulders of the population while the private profits went to the manufacturers. Right from the start the State enabled the capitalists to satisfy the exigencies of limitless production on the part of the time economy by providing extensions to the limited markets. With the creation of the flow methods of mechanised mass-production during the First World War, and with its post-war integration into the capitalist system on a world-wide scale, the duality of market and plant economy became a permanent feature of world monopoly capitalism. It led to the big slump of the 1930s when both economies broke apart to such an extent that the capitalist system itself was threatened. Only Hitler-Germany's whole-hearted adoption of production of non-marketable goods and rearming for the Second World War helped world capitalism off the rock by the international arms race. After the Second World War there was greater awareness on the part of big business of the contradictions bound up with this form of mass-production and threatening a relapse into pre-war conditions. The large corporations evolved a 'planning' strategy centred on a 'break-even-point' as a guidance for balancing the centrifugal tendencies of production against the centripetal tentacles of the market limitations. Still, without the Korean War in the 50s and the Vietnam War of the 60s and 70s, underpinned by the secular inflation, it is more than doubtful that the recurrence of world-wide economic crisis could have been put off until the later 70s.

This brief outline of events serves to emphasise the ever-deepening contradictions of the dual economics which are basic to the nature of monopoly capitalism and which help to explain the increasingly damaging effects of capitalism on society. While the regulatives of the market economy are weakened by manipulation, the growing pressures for continuous production and the time economy of capacity utilisation become the overall leading forces of capitalist development. Market economy, fundamental to commodity production, must be retained if capitalism is to survive, and production economy must be made to exist within the market economy. But these limitations which capitalism must impose upon plant economy for its own continuation should not stop us from analysing the formal structure of production and of Taylorism. So far we have viewed this new economy only as a part of capitalism in its third stage, yet it might harbour potentialities which could assume a vital significance if society were no longer subservient to capitalism. This in no way implies a belief that capitalism is already in a state of transition towards such a future nor that there is any innate necessity for a final breakdown, other than by its revolutionary overthrow. Nevertheless we might remember Marx's remarks in *Grundrisse*

> But within bourgeois society, the society that rests on *exchange value*, there arise relations of circulation as well as of production which are so many mines to explode it. (A mass of antithetic forms of the social unity, whose antithetic character can never be abolished through quiet metamorphosis. On the other hand, if we did not find concealed in society as it is the material conditions of production and the corresponding relations of exchange prerequisite for a classless society, then all attempts to explode it would be quixotic.)[29]

We have retraced the basic roots of commodity production to the separation between labour and societisation (social synthesis) which occurred under the impact of the developing technology of the Iron Age. Capitalism is at the same time the result and the promoter of a re-socialisation of labour. In our belief, monopoly capitalism marks the highest stage of re-socialisation of labour in its state of dependency upon capital.

31

The Necessity for a
Commensuration of Labour

We must now turn to the fundamentals of man's historical existence as a social being. These fundamentals are nowhere stated more convincingly nor more concisely than in a famous letter of Marx to Kugelmann dated 11 July 1868, shortly after the first appearance of volume 1 of *Capital*, when Marx was irked by the lack of comprehension of one of its reviewers.

> The unfortunate fellow does not see that, even if there were no chapter on value in my book, the analysis of the real relationships which I give would contain the proof and demonstration of the real value relation. The nonsense about the necessity of proving the concept of value arises from complete ignorance both of the subject dealt with and of the method of science. Every child knows that a country which ceased to work, I will not say for a year, but for a few weeks, would die. Every child knows too that the mass of products corresponding to the different needs require different and quantitatively determined masses of the total labour of society. That this *necessity* of *distributing* social labour in definite proportions cannot be done away with by the *particular form* of social production, but can only change the *form it assumes*, is self-evident. No natural laws can be done away with. What can change, in changing historical circumstances, is the *form* in which these laws operate. And the form in which this proportional division of labour operates, in a state of society where the interconnection of social labour is manifested in the *private exchange* of the individual products of labour, is precisely the *exchange value* of these products.[30]

The natural law that animals are subjected to is comprised in the ecology and the biology of the species and for them involves no historical change. In application to human existence the same necessity is converted to economic law owing to the labour by which man provided for his livelihood, thereby achieving his assimilation to nature by his own doing. Human labour is subjected to changing historical circumstance through the changing scope of his productive forces in this struggle for assimilation. To him the observance of the economy of this struggle is his law of nature, and the apportioning of his labour power to his different needs is its precondition. But this apportioning in societies which have outgrown the primitive stage where labour takes place within everybody's sight demands some formal commensuration of the socially necessary varieties of labour. Some sort of commensuration of labour then becomes a necessity for every kind of society, societies of appropriation and societies of production alike. Marx makes this very clear in *Grundrisse*, with obvious forethought of socialism:

On the basis of communal production, the determination of time remains, of course, essential. The less time the society requires to produce wheat, cattle, etc., the more time it wins for other production, material or mental. Just as in the case of an individual, the multiplicity of its development, its enjoyment and its activity depends on economization of time. Economy of time, to this all economy ultimately reduces itself. Society likewise has to distribute its time in a purposeful way, in order to achieve a production adequate to its overall needs. . . . Thus economy of time, along with the planned distribution of labour time among the various branches of production, remains the first economic law on the basis of communal production. It becomes law, there, to an even higher degree. However, this is essentially different from the measurement of exchange values (labour or products) by labour time. The labour of individuals in the same *branch of work*, and the various kinds of work, are different from one another not only quantitatively but also qualitatively. What does a solely quantitative difference between things pre- suppose? The identity of their *qualities*. Hence the quantitative measure of labour presupposes the equivalence,* the identity of their quality.[31]

Thus the commensuration of labour, demanded by way of 'a law of nature' for any human society, presupposes a quantification of labour of different kinds or by different individuals. And the fact is that labour, as it occurs in society, is not of itself quantifiable. It is not directly quantifiable in terms of needs, nor needs in terms of labour; neither is labour quantifiable in terms of labour time unless the labour were identical in kind or the actual differences, material or personal were disregarded. Therefore to satisfy the 'law of nature' stated by Marx thereby making human society possible, systems of social economy are needed to operate a commensuration of labour based on a quantification of labour. As Marx suggests, both the commensuration and the quantification of labour can be brought about in different ways, and these differences should be taken into account in distinguishing social formations and their economic systems.

A most significant difference in the modes of commensuration of labour rests upon whether it is brought about indirectly by the exchange process, or directly by the labour process. The exchange process, here, stands for the particular form of societisation on the basis of commodity production. The whole secret and difficulty of Marx's analysis of the commodity and of exchange in the opening chapters of *Capital* lies in the task he sets himself of explaining how the exchange process brings about a social commensuration of labour in the guise of commodity value and of money. The abstractification of labour making for its quantification as the hidden determinant of the exchange proportions of the commodities he declares to be the crucial point (the 'pivotal point') for an understanding of political economy. ' . . . by equating their different products to each other in exchange as values, they equate their different kinds of labour as human labour. They do this without being aware of it.'[32]

To sum up we can enumerate five characteristics of the

---

* The German word is Ebenbürtigkeit, meaning 'equality' by birth, rank or dignity. If Marx had meant 'equivalence' he would have used this term. But he makes an explicit distinction between the commensuration by way of exchange value and the commensuration needed in communal production. I deem the use of the word 'equivalence', reminiscent as it is of exchange, therefore out of place here.

commensuration of labour underlying commodity production in accordance with Marxian teaching:

(1) It takes place in exchange and by the valorisation of money and capital.
(2) It takes place indirectly.
(3) It takes place in an unconscious manner.
(4) It takes place as an outcome of the whole circuit of the social exchange process, and
(5) Above all it applies to the labour 'stored or embodied' in the commodities, or as Marx calls it, to 'dead labour'.

The fourth of these characteristics emphasises that, in effecting the commensuration of labour, commodity exchange provides the social nexus, and that the social nexus operates the commensuration of labour. Marx stresses this, but only as the economic implication of the law of value. My analysis widens the implication to embrace the formation of the abstract intellect. This extension does not, of course, in the least invalidate the Marxian analysis but merely complements it. While Marx exposes the economics of the capitalist class antagonism which is unhinged if the private property rights of capital are abolished, I focus on the division of mental and manual labour, which is another aspect of the same class antagonism. However this aspect of the antagonism does not disappear by the abolition of private capital but will have to be consciously liquidated in the progress of socialist construction as a measuring-rod of its success. This has never been taken into account in the Soviet Union except in words, whereas it forms a central issue in the construction of socialism in China since the victory of the proletarian cultural revolution.

32

The Commensuration of Labour in Action

We must now return to Frederick Winslow Taylor and focus upon his method of 'accurate and scientific study of unit times' declared to be 'by far the most important element in scientific management'. His analysis was done in the service of capital and therefore as a method for speeding labour. Under our viewpoint, however, the method need not serve this objective, nor be wielded by capital as a means of enforcing its control over labour. It could even be a method operated by the workers themselves, although then it would certainly differ substantially from Taylorism. But in order to have a firm base for our own considerations we take as a starting-point the way in which it is practised in monopoly capitalist mass-production.

Taylor's aims in analysing manual operations were, in the first place, to find out how the studied operation can be done with least waste of time and minimal effort and fatigue; then to norm the operation as a composite of strictly repetitive and standard parts; to reduce these parts to the smallest particles or 'units' of motion, assumed to be homogeneous in all manual operations; to time these units with the precision of fractions of a second; finally to use these 'unit times' as a foundation of the job evaluation for fixing correct wage and bonus rates. Some of these features have undergone more or less considerable modifications since the days of Taylor; modifications, however, which mainly serve to make Taylorism more acceptable to the workers – to sell it to them. These are of lesser importance from our point of view. It still is a method of direct time-and-motion study, or, better, of job analysis allowing for the possibility that the 'job' in question could be a collective performance of a highly automated workshop or of a section of it as it is in the measured day-rate system of management.

Our interest lies in the fact that here operations of different qualitative description are being expressed as different multiples of each other in quantitative terms of labour time. We have, in other words, a systematic quantification on standards of uniform time measures and thus a commensuration of labour in the literal meaning of it, over a range of operations. Since Taylor's time these operations have expanded to one industry after another and even to agriculture, mining, transportation and many of the service industries as well as to administration, to clerical work and design.[33] If we compare this mode of commensurating labour with the one effected by the social exchange process as analysed by Marx, it becomes obvious at a glance that both are diametrical opposites to each other in every vital characteristic. The mode initiated by Taylor is:

(1) Rooted in the labour process of production.
(2) It is a direct form of quantification.
(3) It is carried out consciously with the aim of quantification in mind.
(4) It is performed for single particular jobs, each analysed in 'strict isolation', building up in stages to sectional parts and to the entirety of existing or even of projected labour processes, and
(5) Most important of all, it applies to labour in action in contrast to 'dead labour' stored in commodities.

However, an essential reservation must be made in speaking of a system of commensuration of labour of any kind. It must have a character of causal reality in practice and not be merely a calculation existing somewhere on paper. The commensuration of dead labour is given causal reality by the actual performance of acts of exchange. Only by the reality of these acts is it actually carried out and takes shape as the economic laws governing a social system of commodity production, whether capitalist or pre-capitalist. Thus the element of reality in time and space is an indispensable attribute to labour commensuration. In the case of labour in action the step from its mere existence on paper to its existence for society rests in putting the calculation into reality in an actual process of flow production. Only by a conveyor belt in motion does the calculated proportion of labour which it enforces on the workers assume the functional reality of social labour commensuration. Remembering Ford's first installation of flow production, when no preliminary time studies had been made, a commensuration of these jobs nevertheless entered into force with no previous calculations.

We must, of course, remember that the time standards of labour commensuration vary from factory to factory, corresponding to their degree of competitiveness, and even vary within the same factory where the speed of operations is changed at frequent intervals. These different standards set the framework for the production process among monopoly capitalists who, on the one hand, associate to manipulate the markets, and, on the other, work in fierce competition. They must therefore operate the dynamics of their monopolistic economy of production within a framework of market economy to make it fit into a system of social synthesis.

33
The Way to Automation

We have seen how the economy of time not only forces every firm to aim at the uninterrupted continuity of its production process but also to apply the highest possible speed and the greatest economy in the use of constant capital. Competitiveness demands the quickest capital turnover, and this again adds to the pressure for speed of operations. As a result there is a shortening cycle of renewal of plant at a rising level of technology and increased cost. Thereby the proportion of the circulating part of the capital relative to the fixed part tends continuously to rise. Since it is only the circulating part of the productive capital which carries surplus value (cf. *Grundrisse* [34]) the tendency helps to countervail the trend toward a falling rate of profit.

In short, the cumulative pressures of the monopolistic economy of time devolve upon the work force by an ever-increasing speed of operations. Even before the Second World War this speeding had in some cases reached the degree where it surpassed the limits of human capability, and technological agencies were introduced to obtain the required results. One of the first of these, to my knowledge, was the photo-electric cell, or 'electric eye' whose action replaces and exceeds the attention possible by a human person. There is hardly any need to remind ourselves of the stress Marx lays upon this element of human work. 'Apart from the exertion of the working bodily organs, a purposeful will is required for the entire duration of the work. This means close attention.'[35]

To give an example, in the early 1930s the manufacture of razor blades was transformed in Germany from the operations of small-scale cutlers to automated mass-production by large-scale mechanisms relying on photo-electric cells for retaining the flawless blades and rejecting failures at a rate and reliability completely unattainable by a human operator. The Hollerith machine – also based on an electric eye – was in use for office work very much earlier. High speed and mass-production was only made possible by the introduction of such technological agencies in place of human labour power. From the 1950s onwards their use has been enormously extended, tending to make for complete automation of an increasing range of manufacturing processes.

I believe that the essential aspect of this type of automation is ultimately the total replacement of the subjectivity of a human labour-power. By this I mean the entirety of the human person's mental and sensorial activities in the particular jobs of work involved. Details of this replacement have been so frequently and lavishly described that we can spare ourselves the tedium of renewed repetition. It serves our purpose better to quote a very apt, though ironical, passage by Robert Boguslaw:

Our immediate concern, let us remember, is the explication of the operating unit approach to system design, no matter *what* materials are used. We must take care to prevent this discussion from degenerating into a single-sided analysis of the complex characteristics of one type of system material: namely, human beings.

What we need is an inventory of the ways in which human behaviour can be controlled, and a description of some instruments that will help us achieve control. If this provides us sufficient 'handles' on human materials so that we can think of them as one thinks of metal parts, electric power or chemical reactions, then we have succeeded in placing human materials on the same footing as any other materials and can proceed with our problems of system design. Once we have equated all possible materials, one simply checks the catalogue for the price, operating characteristics, and reliability of this material and plugs it in where indicated. . . . There are, however, many disadvantages in the use of human operating units. They are somewhat fragile; they are subject to fatigue, obsolescence, disease and death; they are frequently stupid, unreliable, and limited in memory capacity. But beyond all this, they sometimes seek to design their own system circuitry. This, in a material, is unforgiveable. Any system utilizing them must devise appropriate safeguards.[36]

What is here described, by way of a persiflage, but not far wrong from the true reality, denotes the whole line of monopolistic development of the labour process leading up to automation.

A great deal more automation could be introduced in the capitalist world than is, in fact, carried out. The reason for holding back is not only the excessive cost and rise of overheads attending automation in many cases, but the fact that the extension of automation beyond certain limits is bound to defeat the very end of the whole process, which is to maximise profits. It is easier and safer for monopoly capital to scan the world for cheap and willing labour still available for exploitation. To develop the full potentialities of automation will probably be a task remaining for socialism.

34
The Curse of the
Second-Nature

With the achievement of automation the postulate of the automatism which we described in Part II of this book has reached its final stage. In automation the second nature reigns supreme. Ruled as it is by the logic of appropriation, the second nature cannot enrich itself out of any other source than real nature, and labour is the channel through which it does so. Capital grew fat and mighty by sucking the surplus out of labour. Can it continue to grow fat out of its own products? Capital faces the ultimate contradiction. The labour process has to function for capital as automatism to enable capital to exploit labour. But now the automatism alone remains and labour is discarded. Obviously, labour is fully discarded only in the rarest of cases; as a rule, automation only covers part-processes. And although its scope and its range are increasing, in the great mass of industries the global size of the human work-force still grows, both in the advanced and in the developing countries, even with unemployment forming stagnant pools.

An automated labour process is still a labour process, but a labour process of a completely social scope, social in the terms of a science and a technology resting on the logic of appropriation peculiar to commodity value. The subjectivity of the individual labour-power, the mental, sensorial and nervous functions of an individual while at work, has been replaced by the electronics of automation. Technological devices, in substituting for the workers' personal attributes, emancipate the subjectivity of labour from the organic limitations of the individual and transform it into a social power of machinery. Thus the electronics of an automated labour process act, not for the subjectivity of one worker only, but for all the workers employed in its previous manual stage. Automation amounts to the socialisation of the human labour-power which, in certain aspects, it surpasses in its scope of capability, range of action, its speed, reliability and precision, though only in a restricted and set specialisation.

As Marx traces the evolution of the capitalist mode of production throughout its history he never fails to point to its emancipating effect as well as its evils. Even prior to the employment of machinery, in the period of manufacture: 'When the worker co-operates in a planned way with others, he strips off the fetters of his individuality, and develops the capabilities of his species.'[37] Then when the machine enters the picture: 'The number of tools that a machine-tool can bring into play simultaneously is from the outset independent of the organic limitations that confine the tools of the handicraftsmen.'[38] Similarly as to the gain in power: 'As soon as tools had been converted from being manual implements of a man into the parts . . . of a machine, the motive mechanism also acquired an independent form, entirely emancipated from the restraints of human strength.'[39] Taking into consideration the factory as a whole: 'Along with the tool, the skill of the worker in handling it passes over to the machine. The capabilities of the tool are emancipated from the restraints inseparable from human labour-power.'[40]

Many other indications of this aspect of the capitalist development could be gathered from Marx's writings. The talk of 'emancipation' should of course not evoke illusions. It is not the worker who could ever reap emancipatory benefits under capitalism. The worker is not freed from labour by the machine, but his labour is emptied of its content, as Marx remarks. It is capital that is emancipated from certain barriers which hitherto set limits to the range of the exploitation of labour. As long as science and technology serve the development of the means of production of capital their advance can but be for the enhancement of profits at the expense of the workers:

all means for the development of production undergo a dialectical inversion so that they become means of domination and exploitation of the producers.[41]

Nevertheless, to associate this process with the term 'emancipation' carries an important pointer for the working class. The achievement of socialism does not necessitate scrapping the means of capitalist production to replace them by socialist means. To recognise, with Marx, the potentialities of emancipation in the capitalist machinery means, however much this machinery incorporates the rule of capital over labour,[42] it can be transformed into means of production for socialism once the revolutionary power of the working class has broken the power of capital.

Each step of emancipation is due to the directly social capacity of capital, to its nature as social power in private hands. Automation, however, marks a step of emancipation more significant and far-reaching than any before. Here the worker has not only his work alleviated, he is dismissed from the work himself. Automation, seen by itself, is a creation by the powers of appropriation, those of capital and those of the intellect. This creation must be put into a new relationship with man just as man needs a new relationship to the automating machinery.

We thus have the result that now man would, in principle, have at his disposal production forces which in themselves embrace in their physical reality the socialisation which in the ages of commodity production has grown up in the intellectual work of the human mind – that is, in science. This is a reversal in the relationship between man and his tool. The tools are the repositories of his social potentialities and man can remain an individual using these tools to satisfy his needs and wishes with as yet unforeseeable horizons. It is clear that this assumes socialism in the place of capitalism.

It must, however, be remarked that abolition of private capital by the abrogation of its property rights does not automatically dispose of the antithesis of intellectual and manual labour. If this antithesis remains in being it makes for the continuation of an antagonistic society. Only conscious political action by the revolutionary forces can overcome this obstacle to socialism and make the direct producers the power that masters, handles and develops the means of production. Otherwise the development and disposal of the forces of social production remain the privilege of scientists and technologists, of experts and specialists who, enmeshed with a vast bureaucracy of administrators, carry on a reign of technocracy.

This marks the chief dividing-line between the People's Republic of China and Soviet Russia as the main protagonists of socialism in the world today. The Russians justify their regime as a socialist one on the ground that it guarantees the speediest way to automation, but even this is contended by China where it is argued that the workers must build the automation themselves to suit their own purposes.

The interest of capital to maintain the gap between the advanced and opulent countries and the developing and poverty-stricken is as deep and as permanent as ever. And it will keep a world in being in which that which is possible is hidden by that which is existing. Capital will exert any means at its command to maintain the rule of a logic of appropriation and prevent a rule of the logic of production from restoring man's proper relation to nature on earth. And yet it is the very dialectic of capitalism which creates the conditions for a society of production to arise.

35
The Epoch of Transition

As Marxists we were brought up to think that of all the contradictions inherent in capitalism the one between the ever-increasing social dimension of production and private appropriation is the most fundamental. It expresses the historical trend of the capitalist mode of production and asserts its transient character. This teaching has gained enhanced relevance in monopoly capitalism. With the introduction of flow production the social dimension assumed a specific structural form of its own and henceforth increased in a conclusive manner reaching in our days the size of the giant multi-national corporations. This provides convincing evidence of the importance of the new commensuration of labour in making the development of production and the development of the markets proceed at variance. Their discrepancy creates problems which tend to exceed the controlling power of private capital and demands supplementation by the social resources and power of the State. The epoch in which we live is the epoch of transition which must either lead to socialism or to social disaster.

Science and technology have developed to new forms. But while classical physics is securely based on its mathematical and experimental method, the relativity theory and quantum physics have thrown science into methodological uncertainty. Classical physics in its unchallenged reign shared the lifespan of modern capitalism up to the end of its classical free-market period. Although now relegated to second place, it still has an important role to play and remains an adequate scientific method for a great mass of the technological tasks in the present world, not excluding the socialist parts. Were we then entitled to speak of classical science as 'bourgeois science' as we did in Chapter 20?

Let us be quite clear: methodologically, classical physics has nothing to do with the exploitation of labour by capital. Its findings are valid irrespective of any particular production relations. Inasmuch as it is based on the mathematical and experimental method science is one and one only. Exact science carries objectivity because the elements of the exchange abstraction, which in themselves are entirely of the second nature, have substantial identity with the corresponding elements of real nature owing to the fact that the separation of exchange from use and hence the creation of the exchange abstraction itself happens as an event in time and space in every occurrence of exchange.

On the other hand, looking at nature under the categories of the commodity form, science affords precisely the technology on which hinges the controlling power of capital over production. It cuts up nature piecemeal by isolating its objects of study from the context in which they occur, ignoring nature in its importance as the habitat of society. The environmental conditions are treated as a mass of interfering circumstances which must at all cost be kept out of the experiments. In this way the phenomena are severed from the human world and cut down to recurrent events;

these are defined by mathematical equations signifying the description of immutable 'laws of nature' providing the automatism demanded by capital. True, this deterministic and orthodox concept of natural law has in more recent times been increasingly supplemented by statistical laws and therewith strict necessity by probability. However, the pattern of exact science is still fundamentally that of classical physics.

It is a pattern of science closely connected with the division of intellectual and manual labour. In fact, it forms the hard core of this division since the intellect is the very creation of the exchange abstraction circulating as money and again as capital. The practice of science in the service of capital pays allegiance to an idea of the intellect which is a fetish concept of the human mind seen as the spontaneous source of the non-empirical concepts basic to science. In the framework of this fetishism the science of the mathematical and experimental method is indeed bourgeois science, the scientists pursuing their vital social tasks while being steeped in false consciousness about their function and the nature of science itself. Our attempt to retrace the intellectual powers of conceptual reasoning to the real historical roots in the social systems of commodity production serves the critical liquidation of this fetishism and its epistemological doctrine.

36
Logic of Appropriation and Logic of Production

The basic difference of socialism from capitalism, as seen from our viewpoint, is in the relationship of society to nature. Whereas in capitalism the existing technology serves as machinery for the exploitation of one class of society by another, in socialism it must be made the instrument of the relationship of society to nature. If present advanced technology does not allow for such a change then it must be transformed and freed from the adverse elements and the power structure ingrained in it. To speak with Ernst Bloch, the science and technology of our age rule over nature like 'an occupying army in enemy country', whereas in socialism we must aim to establish 'an alliance of society with nature'.[43] This cannot be done by dispensing with science, but demands the aid of a science backed by the unity of mental and manual work.

Contemporary history offers examples which can be drawn upon to illustrate some features of this fundamental change. It cannot be our intention here to give more than the barest hints of the tenets involved; a detailed examination must be reserved for a separate study. The examples I choose are three: (1) the remarkable enterprise of the Tennessee Valley Authority (T.V.A.) in the U.S.A., (2) a special aspect of the development of socialism in the People's Republic of China, and (3) a negative lesson to be derived from Stalin's 'Plan for the Remaking of Nature' of 1948.

Of the work of the T.V.A. David E. Lilienthal, its first chairman, has given an inspiring report covering the first decade under the significant subtitle *Democracy on the March*.[44] His book is a mine of information deserving scrutiny by present-day students for the positive and the negative features of the project as seen from a socialist viewpoint. The T.V.A. was created in April 1933, at the crest of the wave of Roosevelt's New Deal – the nearest the U.S.A. has ever been to a social revolution.

The catchment basin of the Tennessee River, an area almost the size of England and Scotland combined, utterly eroded and devastated by capitalist exploitation, was, like a patient revived from the brink of death, restored to health and prosperity. Waters once wasted and destructive were controlled for irrigation, electricity, transport, fishing, and pleasure; planned conservation of the soil re-created the fertility of the land; agriculture, industry, forestry, mining, village and town communities flourished. This was a task of combined action upon a region in its entirety, which could not be performed by the isolating strategy of bourgeois science in the service of capital. The fundamental aspects of the project are formulated by Lilienthal right at the beginning of his report as the two governing tenets of the enterprise:

'First, that resource development must be governed by the unity of nature itself.

'Second, that the people must participate actively in that development.

'But if, in the doing, the unity of nature's resources is disregarded, the price will be paid in exhausted land, butchered forests, polluted streams, and industrial ugliness. And if the people are denied an active part in this great task, then they may be poor or they may be prosperous but they will not be free.' We would say they would be the slaves of capitalist exploitation.

Our second example, revolutionary China, of course offers inexhaustible illustrations of society coping with nature as the human habitat and on the basis of socialist democracy. The instance I choose accentuates the unification of mental and manual labour.

Jack Westoby, a former forestry specialist of the International Food and Agricultural Organization (F.A.O.), surveys the progress of afforestation made in China since 1949 'after two millennia of forest depletion'.[45] He heads his article 'Whose Trees?' and analyses the problems involved – embracing not merely the planting of trees but the entire ecology – from the viewpoint: 'To whom does science belong?' The necessity is not to alter the methodological constitution of science to change its character from a bourgeois to a socialist one, but the need is for 'the daily revolution which is making science everybody's business. This is the most important aspect of the evolution of Chinese science.' 'Why have plantings since the mid-sixties been very much more effective than the ones preceding? The heart of the answer . . . has to do with the Cultural Revolution, with the struggle of the masses making science their property. . . . It radiated the available expertise into the countryside, making the special knowledge of forestry science more directly the property of the masses. And it encouraged and helped the peasants to analyse their own experience: to become forestry scientists themselves. New forests are created by the people, not by professional foresters.' Here, in accordance with the teaching of

Mao Tse-tung, science is not discarded; it is, on the contrary, utilised in all its specialised and isolating practices but in a socialist framework and integrated into the context of nature as the human habitat. The use and significance of science changes in this process of transfer to the direct producers. However, it is not a change resulting from a prior decision about the class nature of science, but from the effects of the socialist practice it is made to serve.

In Stalin's famous or notorious 'Plan for the Remaking of Nature'[46] science, and the special science of biology and plant-breeding, was discarded because the isolating method of genetical selection was judged to be bourgeois in essence and incompatible with the alleged Marxian truth of 'dialectical materialism'.[47] Here a science is discarded, not in the light of new research of superior scientific validity, but simply on the strength of a philosophical belief in 'dialectical materialism' regarded as an *a priori* truth. It is well known that the substitute for the orthodox biological science was provided by T. D. Lysenko and that with Stalin's connivance all the geneticists opposing Lysenko were ousted from the Lenin Academy of Agricultural Science of the U.S.S.R. in the Session of July – August 1948. The course of action advocated by Lysenko and adopted by Stalin and the Party proved bogus and condemned the much-boosted plan to failure, entailing considerable damage to Russian agriculture.

Here a project had been conceived for tackling nature as a whole, like the project of the T.V.A. though on a vastly more grandiose scale and by a government professing to be socialist. But while the T.V.A. made the greatest possible use of science and advanced technology, Stalin relied on the doctrine of reflection and the associated materialist metaphysics. There was emphasis on basic democracy in the execution of the plan but the masses did not benefit and the attempt at breaching the division of intellectual and manual labour remained unavailing.

What emerges from these examples is, first, that the science indispensable for socialism is methodologically the same as the science in capitalism; second, that socialism has the means to counteract the properties which, in capitalism, constitute the bourgeois character of this science. These properties are: that the basic categories of science are of the second nature and totally alienated from the qualitative realities of the first nature; that science is compelled to single out its objects as isolates; and that it must be carried out as an intellectual exploit.

All these properties are capable of remedy by the feature, the essential one of socialism, that the people as direct producers must be the controlling masters of both the material and intellectual means of production, and that they act in concert to establish their prosperity within nature in its global unity. For this feature signifies that the material practice of the people in their social exploits commands the need for scientific findings to be integrated into the relationship of society to nature. In the service of capital the findings of science are each of them items in commodity form presented to capital for its exploitation. This position does not alter when a number of such findings are combined to be exploited in their association; whereas in the practice of a socialist project, as evidenced also by the work of the T.V.A., the findings of science never remain single, but are always combined under the logic of production regulating any collective interaction with nature.

The difference then between the status of science in capitalism and in socialism is not in that the logic of science will change from a logic of appropriation to one of production. It is rather that the relationship between them differs. In capitalism the logic of appropriation reigning in the economics of profit-making and in science dominates the logic of production in the manual activities of the wage-labourers, whereas in socialism the relationship is the opposite: that the logic of production animating any socialist project dominates the logic of appropriation of a science belonging to the producers. It cannot, of course, be ruled out that in the long run the logic and method of science will alter as a result of socialist developments. But what is certain to change is the technology taken over from capitalism. And this change will not only be one of the machinery itself but also a change in the manner of producing it. Its construction will increasingly become the work of the direct producers rather than that of professional experts. We can see many examples of this change in China, particularly since the Cultural Revolution. Given a new, qualitatively different technology a new theoretical conception of its mode of working may emerge deepening its understanding and giving it the universality needed for its general social utilisation.[48]

Our considerations in this chapter are based on the assumption of future socialism, transforming the giant social dimensions of present capitalist corporations to collective projects by the people as masters of their destiny. It is not our place here to predict how socialism is to come about in the advanced parts of the world. It is certain, however, that a change of the social system can no longer be spearheaded by an armed uprising of the workers as in the past, since the distribution of armed power is one-sided beyond dispute. On the other hand, what the ruling class is piling up in material arms it is losing morally by its mounting disrepute. It fails increasingly to serve society by providing gainful employment for the people and actively endangers their life by the technological perversions in military and industrial use. Therefore, it ought to be only a question of time until the workers can defeat the ruling system, armed with the political support and the ideological backing of the overwhelming mass of the people. The purpose of a study like the present must be seen against such a background.

PART IV

HISTORICAL MATERIALISM AS METHODOLOGICAL POSTULATE

37

The Theory of Reflection and its Incompatibilities as a Theory of Science

The theory of knowledge and of science prevalent among some Marxists and particularly those paying allegiance to the Soviet Union is the theory of reflection. While I fully recognise the political importance of this theory and its ideological purpose for use against idealism and positivism, I consider its theoretical value to be nil. In fact it has the damaging effect of mitigating against all serious historical-materialist investigation of the phenomena of cognition. The theory of reflection is not historical materialistic but is an offshoot of natural materialism.

These remarks will, of course, arouse violent contradiction among reflectionists, and pronounced boldly in this way they may appear incorrect. But are they really so? I would answer those who reject my statement that I am aware that the reflectionists embrace more into their epistemology of the sciences than mere external nature; they also take into account historical and social factors. Nevertheless, these additional factors are only arrayed to make the reflection of nature appear more plausible. Hence, what they serve to support is the assertion of a reflection of nature. Or, put another way: remove the reflection of nature from the whole complex argument, then all the subsidiary elements would lose their meaning. Even taking into account Todor Pawlow's seven hundred and fifty pages[1] presenting the theory of reflection there only remains the assertion that the formation, method and objectivity of science are explained by the scientific mind reflecting its object of cognition as it exists in nature. This is natural materialism and no amount of elaboration can ever succeed in changing it into historical materialism.

Of course, there is nothing wrong in natural materialism so long as it is applied to phenomena of nature; but is consciousness one of these? The only sort of consciousness which forms under the direct impact of nature is the instinct of animals. Whether or not this could rightly be called consciousness is a matter for debate. Alexeyev Nikolayev Leontyev,[2] one of the stalwarts of the reflection theory, would probably raise no objection since he reduces the theory to the level of physiology, at least as a starting-point. However, I would regard this of very little value for the elucidation of the phenomena of consciousness with which our investigations in this book are concerned.

Cognitive faculties such as Greek philosophy, mathematics and the exact sciences are clearly human manifestations, as is the whole field of conceptual thought from which they arise. To understand the human world Marx created historical materialism. The vital point for him in this respect was the realisation that 'it is men's social being that determines their consciousness' – their *social being*, not nature, not *natural being*. When a theorist of reflection speaks of 'nature', 'external nature' or man's own 'internal nature' he is animated by ideas already determined by his social being. His whole thought about reflective consciousness is an ideology of a particular social class and historical epoch.

Moreover there is another major objection to the theory of reflection. I understand 'natural science' in the sense of the mathematical and experimental method emerging from the scientific revolution of the seventeenth century. This is modern bourgeois science, inextricably linked with the capitalist mode of production. It presents a mathematically exact knowledge of nature from sources other than manual labour and other than experience gained from such work. Natural science in this sense is essentially founded upon methodological concepts of a non-empirical character, which make mathematics applicable to observable phenomena of nature, such as, for instance, Galileo's and Newton's concept of inertial motion. To try to explain the foundations of modern bourgeois science from a reflection of nature is incompatible with the non-empirical character of these foundations. It implies a misreading of the methodological tenets of modern science. The theory of reflection may be fruitful when referring to empirical knowledge based on a unity of head and hand, as in the case of handicraftsmen, but modern science evolved when this kind of knowledge became ineffectual. The hallmark of mathematically based thinking that took the place of craftsmanship is its intellectual character radically divided from manual practice.

I regard my argument against the theory of reflection as applied to natural science of major political importance. From it must follow the conclusion that the enactment of science in unbroken continuation of its tradition as practised in the capitalist world is incompatible with socialism. It may well be that science and scientific technology have not yet reached a stage where a socialist transformation can emerge from the bourgeois tradition. But unless the development leading towards this stage is carried under the revolutionary impetus of the proletarian forces, as appears to be the case in China, then socialist transformation, when it becomes due or overdue, will require a proletarian revolution to overturn a hardened techno-cratic class-rule based on intellectual privilege.

The theory of reflection simulates the neutrality of science and technology towards social class, and assumes indifference to social order. By these characteristics it is marked as an ideology of technocracy, not of socialism. Its statements concerning the source of knowledge are assertions which by their very nature are unproven and unprovable. To support them and lend them a semblance of conviction the theory as a whole is fortified by certain generalised pronouncements supporting materialism. They run somewhat like this: materialism, as a rational stand-point, demands that the external material world exists inde-pendent of any consciousness; that, as a general truth, matter is prior to mind and being is prior to consciousness; so, clearly, consciousness reflects the external world, and it reflects being; hence, ideas and thoughts are not only alleged to derive from material reality but actually do so, and all that is required is the explanation of *how* this occurs. Thus when you ask a reflectionist how he knows that a specific idea is a reflection of being he answers by reiterating the same contention in the guise of a prime truth. I consider this a feat of dogmatic reasoning completely at odds with Marxian thinking which is undogmatic and critical to the core.

In the *Philosophical Dictionary of the German Democratic Republic* (*Wörterbuch der Philosophie*) [3] the case for the theory of reflection is argued in a way which amounts to burking the main question. The human person is presented as equipped with sense organs doing the service of impersonal measuring and registering instruments such as are indispensable for scientific experiments. Here, science, far from being explained, is introduced as a given state of affairs. The historical fact that people living in commodity-producing societies develop a social form of thinking in non-empirical abstracts constituting a pure intellect divided from their bodily activities – this fact is taken for granted and treated as though it were part of human nature. We would all agree that sensations perceived by persons through their individual sense organs are personally sensed, and differently so by different persons. But this truth does not seem to occur to the leading theorists of reflection in the German Democratic Republic. One has the impression that the difference between an individual and a robot is but one of degree. True, scientific man is an individual who, upon entering his laboratory, abdicates his subjectivity of a person and with it the entirety of his existential personal condition, but how does a living person change into this extraordinary status of scientific man? This, surely, is an important part of the question that a theory of science is called upon to answer. This criticism of reflectionism is cogently reasoned in an excellent study by Bodo von Greiff. [4]

But this is no wholesale condemnation of the theory of reflection as such. It only contests any claim for it as a critical theory of science. I consider it unfit to challenge philosophical epistemology and to perform the critical liquidation of the bourgeois fetishism of science and scientific technology, which is a prime necessity to achieve socialism as an outcome of a revolutionary liquidation of the bourgeois class-rule. Socialism demands the disappearance of the division between mental and manual labour and I reiterate that the reflection theory never probes into the socio-historical matrix of this division and completely disregards the social foundation of this formation of the intellect. A construction of true socialism in our western setting is, in my view, a near impossibility without a correct historical-materialist understanding of science and of the relationship of mental and manual labour.

However, in many other fields except that of science the theory of reflection does invaluable service. For an understanding of the psychology of everyday life it is indispensable, as Georg Lukacs has shown. And it has at least relative merits in the theory of aesthetics. What useful role it can play for understanding the labour process of production and of its management has been demonstrated in the comprehensive study of Winfried Hacker on the *General Psychology of Labour and Engineering*.[5]

38
Materialism versus Empiricism

One of the objections Marxists frequently encounter in academic circles is that the whole juxtaposition of 'social existence (or social being)' to 'consciousness' amounts to a naïve ontologism. What do we know of social existence except through our own consciousness of it? And how is it possible to guard against the hypostatisation of all manner of ideas, preconceptions and standards of value in our approach and our description of what we think is 'social existence'? Yet we claim to judge and criticise all ideas, including our own, in the light of their determination from 'outside' consciousness. Not a single step could we take in carrying out our proclaimed principle without having to beg it. Before starting on our task we need a critical sifting of our own assumptions, and this necessarily requires a *prima philosophia* which Aristotelians seek in ontology, Kantians in epistemology. Thus, before we can start to follow out the postulate of materialism we find ourselves landed in idealism.

This objection must be met; it is no futile argument. In actual fact it is a precise description of what happens to the non-materialist bourgeois historians and sociologists. And for us Marxists it is in the countering of this argument that we strike the dividing-line between us and empiricism.

The entire profession of academic philosophy swears by the axiom that 'no empirical fact can ever prevail against an argument of logic'. The world of these empirical facts does not yield the normative standards on which they could be judged. To decide upon these standards is the exclusive prerogative of the epistemologists. On this both the epistemologists and the empiricists are agreed. It is an error to present the philosophical idealists and the prophets of empiricism as opponents to each other. They both play the same game, although they have separate parts in it.

It is essential to realise that Marx does not recognise this disjunction between 'logic' and 'empirical fact'. In his method he cuts across the traditional antithesis, and the important point is that he does so on strictly critical standards of thinking.

39
Marx's Own Object Lesson

Marx's *Capital* bears the sub-title *Critique of Political Economy*, the same as formed the main title of the earlier study. We have already quoted Marx in the meaning of the term 'political economy': 'Let me point out once for all that by classical political economy I mean all the economists who, since the time of William Petty, have investigated the real internal framework (Zusammenhang) of bourgeois relations of production. . . .'[6] Thus methodologically the subject-matter of Marx's critique is not the historical reality of this or that form of social existence but, in the first instance, a particular mode of consciousness – namely, that of political economy; it is thoughts, not things. It is the concepts of 'value', 'capital', 'profit', 'rent', etc., as he found them defined and discussed in the writings of the economists. He does not deal directly with realities, does not elaborate concepts of his own which, as 'correct' ones, he would oppose to the 'false' ones of the economists. His approach is characteristically different. It is an approach to reality, but by way of the 'critique' of the historically given consciousness.

Following the Smith – Ricardian concept of 'value' Marx defines as 'commodity' the reality to which it refers: it is as 'an immense collection of commodities' that capitalist society 'appears',[7] appears that is, as seen through the spectacles of the established mode of thinking. Marx then analyses commodity (not value) insisting all the time on finding in it the correspondence to the concepts and distinctions of the economists, and what he finds is – the historical origin of the seemingly timeless concept of 'value'. It is on this purely critical line of procedure, on the standards of the very concepts he is out to criticise, that he establishes the determination of a given mode of consciousness by social existence, and thereby, as the intended result, succeeds in uncovering the true reality of that social existence.

Thus, far from hypostatising any concepts and assumptions, Marx, on the contrary, starts out from suspecting everybody's ideas and notions, his own included. They are the notions and ideas which the world of ours imposes upon us. To the empiricist they are the prime material from which he coins the 'truth'. Marx looks upon them all as potentially false, as the deceit of our world just as likely as a glimpse of truth.

The truth about our world is concealed to everybody under the spell of his false consciousness. When our academic opponents ask what we know of that social existence which we oppose to consciousness our answer would be: we know of it as little as you do. But we know how to find out. The way to do so is to trace the genetical origin of any current ideas and concepts, on the very standards of them. Social existence is that which we shall find determines these ideas and concepts.

Read as a statement of an inherent truth Marx's sentence is

worth less than nothing. It is a link-up of two questions each begging the other. To know how to judge consciousness we are referred to social existence, but to know about social existence we are referred to consciousness. Understood, however, as a methodological postulate the sentence says everything. For this interacting reference is precisely the movement we have to carry out in our actual search. The Marxist method in *Capital* is the continuous reference of concept to reality, of reality to ideology. Reality is put on trial upon the summons of established theory, and, in the face of reality, theory stands convicted as necessary, and necessarily, false consciousness.

40

Necessary False Consciousness

This term is an all-important one in historical materialism. The various notions and ideas men form in their historical world and surroundings are of very different weight and consistency. Some are formed in a slipshod manner, held one day and dropped or modified the next. Some are cranky and neurotic, peculiar to one individual or another. Some are freakish, based on muddled thinking. Very little of value to a materialist can, as a rule, be gained from tracing ideas of this kind to their genetical condition. If the ideas are accidental themselves, their genetical basis is accidental too. The same is true resulting from a personal bias for this or that political or social cause. They do not reflect any of the necessities and impersonal forces governing the historical course of our social world. In order to penetrate into the foundations of this world and to learn how it holds together and how it could be changed effectively we must seize upon 'necessary false consciousness' as subject-matter for materialistic critique.

Before Marx started on the writing of *Capital* he spent fifteen years reading the whole of economic literature available in the British Museum. These studies were on the line of purely inherent criticism of the theories as they stood, and were aimed at sifting the logically sound, unimpeachable core of economic thinking from anything traceable to faulty argument. The faulty parts he discarded and only on the hard, systematically valid core of the science did he base his *Critique of Political Economy*. With these critical siftings Marx filled copious notebooks, an important selection of which was posthumously edited by Kautsky in three volumes as *Theorien über den Mehrwert* (*Theories of Surplus-Value*).[8] According to Marx's own original plans they were to form the fourth volume of *Capital*.

Necessary false consciousness, then, is not faulty consciousness. It is, on the contrary, logically correct, inherently incorrigible consciousness. It is called false, not against its own standards of truth, but as against social existence. Roughly, the Marxist approach to historical reality can be understood as answering the question: what must the existential reality of society be like to necessitate such and such a form of consciousness? Consciousness fit to serve as the theme of enquiry of this kind must be socially valid, free from accidental flaws and personal bias. Necessary false consciousness, then, is (1) necessary in the sense of faultless systematic stringency.

Necessary false consciousness is (2) necessarily determined genetically. It is necessary by historical causation. This is a truth of existence, not immanently inferable from the consciousness concerned. It is the truth specific of materialism.

Necessary false consciousness is (3) necessarily false consciousness determined genetically so as to be false by necessity. Its falseness cannot be straightened out by means of logic and by conceptual adjustments. Historical materialism rejects the Kantian idea of epistemology as ultimate *arbiter philosophiae*. Consciousness is not the function of a 'mind' capable of absolute self-criticism on lines of pure logic. Pure logic itself does not control, but is controlled by, its timeless idea of the truth; of this idea itself there is no immanent criticism or confirmation. Necessary false consciousness is false, not as a fault of consciousness, but by fault of the historical order of social existence causing it to be false. The remedy is in a change of this order, a change which would remove powerful and deep-rooted characteristics upon which that causation can be proved to rest. Marx lays great stress upon the fact that his critical disclosure of the fetish character of the value concept by no means does away with the spell of this concept which commodity production must exercise as long as it is allowed to remain in being. Man, in the social sense, is not wrong; he is deceived. He is innocent of his necessary false consciousness, and no amount of cruelty and slaughter ensuing from it among men can impair the eligibility of mankind for fighting its way through to a classless society.

Lastly, necessary false consciousness is (4) necessary pragmatically. It is necessary for the perpetuation of the social order in which it holds sway over men's minds. Where this order is based on social class rule the necessary false consciousness is the consciousness needed by the ruling classes to maintain their rule. On the other hand the false consciousness of ruling class is necessary false consciousness only so long as their rule is itself historically necessary and continues to be irreplaceable for reasons of the given stage of development of the productive forces. Necessary false consciousness has its roots, not in the class struggle, but in those conditions of historical necessity out of which class antagonism itself results. This might give rise to distinguishing necessary false consciousness from ideology understood in a narrow sense as accessory to class struggle. Marx has proved the value concept, for instance, to be the fetish concept of the form of commodity, and commodity exchange to precede the rise of class society. So long as a certain system of social class rule is historically necessary and irreplaceable for the reasons given the false consciousness of the ruling classes is truly representative of the interests of mankind. Political economy lost its innocence and intellectual integrity only when, in 1830, the illusion broke and the class character of bourgeois society became patent even to the bourgeoisie itself. The events of that year 'sounded the death knell of scientific bourgeois economics'.[9] The 'bourgeois vulgar economics' which followed was 'no longer of scientific, but only of historical interest'.[10] Bourgeois class consciousness, in other fields just as much as in economics, came to mean, not false, but falsified consciousness. This kind of class consciousness (the only one that vulgar Marxists seem able to grasp) is, to Marx, a subject not of critique but of contempt. Being no longer necessary false consciousness it is useless for his methodical purpose.

41

The Philosophical Issue

The reality, then, to which Marx critically opposes the various forms of consciousness of men is the historical one of their own social existence. It is not 'matter' or the 'external material world independent of any consciousness'. Our notions of things and the concepts in which we undertake their systematisation are historical products themselves. So are science, mathematics, natural philosophy, etc. It is for the historical materialist to account for the rise as well as the objective validity of science in history, not for the logic of natural science as a logic reflected from nature to supply the principles of historical materialism.

To reason about the world's existence is not one of a historical materialist's commitments. If ever he finds himself involved in arguments of this nature, the line to take is the historical-materialist critique of the standards of thinking on which the world's existence ever came to be questioned. But for a materialist to embark on dogmatic speculation of this style himself to combat idealism is like throwing oneself in the fire in order to extinguish it. The contrast between Marxist materialism and idealism is much more fundamental than that. It is between the Marxian mode of thinking and the whole of dogmatic traditional thinking, idealistic and materialistic. In fact, the issue can be expressed by the contrast of two incompatible conceptions of the truth itself.

Dogmatic thinking, in all its variants, is pledged to the conception of the truth as timeless; Marxist materialism conceives the truth as timebound. Now, under a timeless conception of the truth, idealism is the only consistent standpoint of thinking. If the truth is timeless the spatio-temporal world cannot be ultimately real and the standards of distinction of the true and untrue, i.e. the standards of logic, must be of a transcendental, extra-temporal order. Under the conception of the truth as timebound, *per contra*, materialism is the only consistent standpoint of thinking. And, conversely, materialism is consistent with itself in method and doctrine only as a quest for timebound truth. Such truth is dialectical as it changes in its attainment.

Timebound truth is an existential, not a cognitive, ideal (the term 'existential' understood on a social scale, not the individual one of so-called 'existentialism'). It is a truth of being, not of thinking. The predicates of 'false' or 'correct' are used by Marx, of consciousness in relation to the social reality of its class-holders, not to a concept in relation to an 'object of cognition'. The qualification of that existential reality as 'social' derives from the fact that no individual ever commands the conditions of his own existence.

Hitherto in history social existence has always been such as to necessitate false consciousness. Fulfilment of the ideal of timebound truth would be through the creation of a kind of social order allowing for correct consciousness. Such a social order could, by factual implication, only be a classless one. It would still imply continuous change and not, as by the inconsistency of Hegel's idealism, imply changelessness. The historical potentiality of such an order and the way of its political realisation are explored by accounting for the necessary false consciousness in present and past history. Historical, as distinct from immanent, critique of given forms of consciousness is, thus, the theoretical part of the practical quest for timebound truth; it implies the unity of theory and practice. In this quest the postulate of timebound truth, which is for social consciousness to be in keeping with social being, is the critical principle guiding the road towards social classlessness, the 'socialist road', as say the Chinese. This should make it abundantly clear that this postulate must never be presented in a dogmatic form as a hypostasis, lest the rational foundation be taken away from the materialist position.

Natural science, like mathematics, mathematical physics, etc., is a functional part of a particular form of the social life-process. Its logic is based on the abstraction from our own timebound existential condition, or, as we have said, on the abstraction of society from itself. It is from this abstraction, not from any absolute root and spontaneous 'intellectual' font, that the logic of science derives its character of timelessness. There is, in other words, a timebound cause for timeless logic. In this manner of thinking, it must be said, we understand dialectical materialism and historical materialism as synonymous terms. From the materialistic standpoint, human history is part of natural history and nature is a historical, evolutionary process. As Marx put it in the opening pages of *The German Ideology*: 'We know only of one single science, the science of history!'[11]

42

The Essentially Critical Power of Historical Materialism

Turning now to our own treatment of the intellectual formation of societies based on commodity production we can safely claim that our approach is historical materialistic. We do not merely assert that cognitive concepts are derivatives from material being, we actually derive them one by one from being, not the being of external nature and the material world, but from the *social being* of the historical epochs in which these concepts arise and play their part.

I maintain, moreover, that this derivation has its demonstrative strength in the fact that it satisfies historical materialism in its capacity of a methodological postulate. In the entire tradition of theoretical philosophy grounded in these concepts themselves, from classical antiquity down to our own times, it is regarded as an absolute impossibility that these concepts could ever be derived from spatio-temporal reality. They are severed from such reality by an insuperable gap; taken in their own logical meaning they are universal and abstract, containing no vestige of the world of sense-perception. And yet they carry all the knowledge of the external world that bears conceptual certainty for us. To try to challenge the logically unshakeable conviction of this philosophical reasoning by the materialistic contention that our ideas, including the non-empirical concepts of the pure intellect, are nevertheless derivable from the world in time and space, would not only be utterly lost on these philosophers but, in their eyes, amount to a self-avowal of philosophical ineptness. Any candidate advancing such a proposition in his philosophical examination would certainly fail, or be regarded as a psychiatric curiosity. If he quoted as his authority a person by the name of Marx, he might at best evoke the response: 'Well then, prove that it is as you say or else never repeat the like again!'

Hence, our most elementary convictions as Marxists and historical materialists count for nothing unless they can be proved to be true – true in a way to convince even one of those philosophical archetypes if, indeed, he could allow himself to be so open-minded. For historical materialism, then, to be the political weapon in the proletarian class-struggle which Marx intended it to be, we must think of it, not in terms of a doctrine or of a world-view (Weltanschauung) or any other dogmatic fixture, but purely as a methodological postulate.

In the preface to the first edition of *Capital* Marx speaks of 'My standpoint from which the development of the economic formation of society is viewed as a process of natural history',[12] and this is, indeed, the only standpoint fully consistent with a materialist conception of history. But he also explains that 'in the analysis of economic forms neither microscopes nor chemical reagents are of assistance. The power of abstraction must replace both.'[13] Although we move in the field of natural history we move in a part of it where only argument of reason can lead us to the truth of the facts. Among these facts we have chosen the conceptual mode of thought and its sequels as our subject of investigation and we would claim that the Marxian standpoint applies as much to the intellectual formation of society as it does to the economic one. And, like Marx, we have to revert to our powers of abstraction to carry on the argument of reason required to arrive at the essence of our subject-matter. What power of conviction can we rely upon that our argument of reason may carry?

The conceptual mode of thought arose in history as the basis of intellectual labour inherently divided from manual labour. Intellectual labour of this kind has one common and all-pervading mark: the norm of timeless universal logic. This is a characteristic which makes it incompatible with history, social or natural. Timeless concepts are ahistorical in their meaning and present themselves as historical miracles like the 'Greek miracle' actually so-called for starting conceptual reasoning in Western history. Of course, this ahistorical mode of thinking is itself a historical phenomenon. And so long as its timeless and non-empirical concepts fail to be understood historically, history itself remains incomprehensible. Our analysis has shown, however, that the timelessness of the separate intellect is necessary false consciousness which conceals the historical origin of its constitutive concepts and, consequently, their historical limit. The features characteristic of 'pure reason', the *noûs*, the *intellectus purus*, are objectively deceptive. The true nature of the abstract intellect is, from its appearance to itself, totally unrecognisable. Despite the impression to the contrary its abstractness is not grounded in an intellectual origin, nor is its universality, nor its logical virginity, nor its sublime integrity or even divinity. Belief in an unbridgeable gap severing the intellectual world from the world in time and space is erroneous, but is not caused by personal and subjective deception, but by an unavoidable illusion.

We have been able to disclose the origin of the pure intellectual concepts from the spatio-temporal reality of social being, their character as reflections of the abstraction enshrined in money, hence their nature as offshoots from the reification upon which hinges the cohesion of exchange society, their essential use as forms of socialised thinking, their antithetic relation to manual labour, their accessory link with the class division of society.

These insights into the true nature of the intellectual formation of bourgeois society are accessible only to historical materialism owing to the critical character of its method. The truth revealed on the strength of this standpoint of thinking is not impartial, it is utterly revolutionary. It critically liquidates all the credence on which the ruling classes must rely for the maintenance of their rule. It is calculated to prove the potentiality of social classlessness. The convincing strength that our investigation may be able to claim does not rest exclusively with the logical and genetic derivation of the abstract intellect and its cognitive powers; it is also helped by the degree of comprehensibility that human history gains in the process. The certainty attaching to historical materialistic enquiry, in other words, attaches to the reciprocal reference of consciousness to social being and of social being to consciousness that we pointed out as the essence of Marx's basic methodological principles. Above all, it must be seen that it is not the recourse to the acclaimed neutrality of intellect and intellectual judgement but, on the contrary, the revolutionary commitment of our exposition that yields the truth.

Notes and References

PREFACE

1. Alfred Seidel, *Bewußtsein als Verhängnis*, aus dem Nachlaß herausgegeben von Hans Prinzhorn (Consciousness as Fatality, posthumous papers edited by Hans Prinzhorn) (Bonn: Verlag Friedrich Cohen, 1927).
2. Alfred Sohn-Rethel, *Ökonomie und Klassenstruktur des deutschen Faschismus* (Economics and Class-Structure of German Fascism) (Frankfurt/Main: Suhrkamp, 1974).
3. They are: an article in *Modern Quarterly*, vol. 3, no. 1 (Winter 1947/8); two lectures given in the Humbolt University, Berlin, published in *Academy Journal* (*Wiss. Zeitschr. Humb. Univ.*, Ged.-Sprachwiss. R. X. (1961); an article in *Marxism Today* (Apr 1965); and an approving mention in the preface to the magnificent work of George Thomson, *The First Philosophers* (London: Lawrence & Wishart, 1955).

INTRODUCTION

1. Karl Marx, *Economic and Philosophic Manuscripts of 1844*, trans. Martin Milligan (Moscow, 1961).
2. Alfred Schmidt, *Der Begriff der Natur in der Lehre von Marx* (The Concept of Nature in the Theory of Marx) (Frankfurter Beiträge zur Soziologie, Nr. 11, 1962).
3. Max Horkheimer, *The Eclipse of Reason* (London: Oxford University Press, 1947) p. 59.
4. Marx, 'Critique of the Gotha Programme', *Selected Works* (London: Lawrence & Wishart, 1943) pp. 566 ff.
5. Marx, 'Preface to A Contribution to the Critique of Political Economy' (of 1859), *Selected Works*, p. 356.
6. Marx, *Capital*, vol. 1 (Harmondsworth: Penguin Books, 1976) p. 162.
7. Immanuel Kant, *Kritik der reinen Vernunft* (Critique of Pure Reason) (Großherzog Wilhelm-Ernst Ausgabe, vol. 3, im Insel-Verlag, 1908).
8. Marx, 'Preface . . .', op. cit. p. 357.

PART I

1. Marx, *Capital*, vol. 1 (Harmondsworth: Penguin Books) pp. 174–5 (n.).
2. Kant, op. cit.
3. F. Engels, *Ludwig Feuerbach and the Outcome of Classical German Philosophy*, (The Marxist-Leninist Library) (London, Lawrence & Wishart, 1941).
4. Marx, *Capital*, postface to 2nd edn, p. 103.
5. Marx, *Theses on Feuerbach*; cf. Engels, op. cit., appx, p. 73.
6. Marx and Engels, *The German Ideology*. The passage I quote was crossed out by Marx in the manuscript and not printed in the English edition which I possess.
7. Marx, *Capital*, vol. 1, p. 166.
8. Louis Althusser, *Lire le Capital* (Paris: Maspero, 1965 and 1966) vol. 1, p. 51 (italic by Althusser).
9. Marx, *Capital*, vol. 1, p. 733.
10. Ibid. p. 187.
11. Ibid. p. 138.
12. Ibid. pp. 173–4.
13. Ibid. p. 181.
14. Ibid. pp. 166–7.
15. Ibid. p. 168.
16. I. Kant, *Beantwortung der Frage: Was ist Aufklärung?* (of 1784) (The Answer to the Question: What is Enlightenment?) (Großherzog Wilhelm-Ernst Ausgabe, Bd I) pp. 161 ff.
17. Marx, *Capital*, vol. 1, p. 182.
18. Ibid. p. 178.
19. Bertrand Russell, *Human Knowledge: Its Scope and Limits* (London: Allen & Unwin, 1966) p. 191.
20. Marx, *Capital*, vol. 1, p. 190.
21. Ibid. p. 182.
22. Ibid. pp. 166–7 and p. 167 (n.).
23. Ibid. p. 168.
24. Marx's letter to Kugelmann of 11 July 1868 in *Selected Correspondence of Marx and Engels* (London: Lawrence & Wishart, 1941) p. 246.
25. Marx, *Capital*, vol. 1, pp. 729 and 730.
26. Ibid. p. 733.
27. Marx, *Grundrisse* (Harmondsworth: Penguin Books, 1973) p. 141.
28. F. Engels, *Origin of the Family* (London: Lawrence & Wishart, 1943) pp. 198 f.
29. Ibid. p. 186.
30. G. W. F. Hegel, *Vorlesungen über die Geschichte der Philosophie*

(Lectures on the History of Philosophy) (Leipzig: Verlag Philipp Reclam jun., 1971) vol. 1, p. 390.

31. Francis M. Cornford, *Plato and Parmenides*, Parmenides' *Way of Truth* and Plato's *Parmenides*, trans. with an introduction and a running commentary (London: Kegan Paul, Trench & Trubner, 1939) p. 29.

32. Hermann Diels, *Fragmente der Vorsokratiker* (Berlin, 1903) p. 119.

33. Cornford, op. cit. p. 34.

34. Cf. ibid. p. 26.

35. Marx, *Capital*, vol. 1, p. 494 (n.).

36. Francis M. Cornford, *From Religion to Philosophy* (London: Edward Arnold, 1912) p. 5.

37. George Thomson, *The First Philosophers* (London: Lawrence & Wishart, 1955) p. 228.

38. Marx, *Capital*, vol. 1, p. 494 (n.).

39. Ibid. p. 165.

PART II

1. Marx, *Capital*, vol. 1, pp. 283–4.

2. Ibid. p. 643.

3. Ibid. p. 647.

4. Thomson, in his book *The First Philosophers* (London: Lawrence & Wishart, 1955), has described the social formation of the Bronze Age civilisations with such clarity and concision that I rely on his work and also refer the reader to it.

5. Joseph Needham, *Science and Civilisation in China*, vol. 3: *Mathematics and the Sciences of the Heavens and the Earth* (Cambridge: Cambridge University Press, 1959).

6. Siegfried Schott, *Altägyptische Festdaten* (Mainz: Akademie der Wissenschaft und der Literatur, Abhandlungen der geistes- und sozialwissenschaftlichen Klasse, Jg 1950, Nr 10).

7. Richard A. Parker, *The Calendars of Ancient Egypt* (Chicago: University of Chicago Press, 1950), Studies in Ancient Oriental Civilisation, no. 26.

8. Thomson, op. cit. p. 182.

9. Engels, *Origin of the Family* (London: Lawrence & Wishart, 1940) p. 209.

10. Ibid. pp. 120–5.

11. Thomson, op. cit. p. 194.

12. Marx, *Capital*, vol. 1, p. 165.

13. Benjamin Farrington, *Science in Antiquity* (Oxford: Oxford University Press, 1969) pp. 17–20.

14. Thomson, op. cit. p. 184.

15. Ibid. pp. 204–5.

16. *Capital*, vol. 1, p. 172.

17. Ibid. pp. 452–3 (n.).

18. Concise and illuminating on this whole aspect of the Middle Ages is S. Lilley, *Men, Machines and History* (London: Lawrence & Wishart, 1965).

19. Rodney Hilton, *The English Peasantry in the Later Middle Ages* (Oxford: Clarendon Press, 1975). Also article 'Origins of Capitalism', in *History Workshop: a Journal of Socialist Historians* (London: Pluto Press, 1976).

20. Hilton, 'Origins of Capitalism', in op. cit. p. 21.

21. Dorothea Oschinsky, *Walter of Henley and other Treatises on Estate Management and Accounting* (Oxford: Clarendon Press, 1971). See also on the same subject H. G. Richardson, 'Business Training in Medieval Oxford', *American Historical Review*, vol. 46.

22. Moritz Cantor, *Vorlesungen über Geschichte der Mathematik* (Lectures on the History of Mathematics), 4 vols (Leipzig: 1880–1908).

23. Albrecht Dürer, *Unterweisung der Messung mit Zirkel und Richtscheit* (Instructions of Measurement with Compass and Ruler), hrsg. (ed.) von Alfred Peltzer (Munich: 1908 and 1970); hier ist der Text um einiges gekürzt und dem neueren Sprachgebrauch angepaßt (the text here is somewhat abbreviated and adapted to modern usage).

24. Cantor, op. cit. vol. 2, p. 429.

25. Leonardo Olschki, *Die Literatur der Technik und der angewandten Wissenschaften vom Mittelalter bis zur Renaissance*, als Bd 1 der Geschichte der neusprachlichen wissenschaftlichen Literatur (The Literature of Technology and the Applied Sciences from the Middle Ages to the Renaissance, as vol. 1 of The History of the Vernacular Scientific Literature) (Leipzig: 1919).

26. Johan Kepler, *Harmonices Mundi* (Lincii Austriae, 1619).

27. Dürer, op. cit. pp. 47 ff.

28. Marx, *Capital*, vol. 1, p. 292.

29. Ibid. pp. 489–90.

30. Ibid. pp. 548–9.

31. Ibid. pp. 501–3.

32. Alexandre Koyré, 'Galileo and the Scientific Revolution of the 17th Century', in *Philosophical Review*, vol. 52 (1943). This essay draws on the author's *Études Galiléennes*, 3 vols (Paris: Hermann, 1966). There are also his *Newtonian Studies* (Chicago: University of Chicago Press Paperback, 1965); *Du Monde clos à l'Univers infini* (Paris: Presses Universitaires de France, 1962); and a most

interesting collection of essays, *Études d'Histoire de la Pensée Scientifique* (Paris: Presses Universitaires de France, 1966), besides his *Études d 'Histoire de la Pensée Philosophique* (Paris: Presses Universitaires de France, 1967).

33. Galileo Galilei, *Discorsi*, ed. Hans Blumenberg (Frankfurt am Main: Insel Verlag, 1965).

34. Koyré, art. cit., *Phil. Rev.*

35. Russell, *Human Knowledge; Its Scope and Limits*, op. cit.

36. See above, Part I, Chapter 9 (c), p. 70.

37. Marx, *Capital*, vol. 1, p. 439.

38. Russell, op. cit. pp. 17 and 30.

39. F. Engels, *Anti-Dühring* (London: Lawrence & Wishart, 1934) p. 71.

40. Bertrand Russell, *History of Western Philosophy* (London: Allen & Unwin, 1946) p. 630.

41. Marx, *Economic and Philosophic Manuscripts of 1844* (Moscow: Foreign Languages Publishing House, 1961) p. 151.

42. We find the same words or cognate ones in a famous footnote in *Capital*, vol. 1, p. 494: 'The weaknesses in the abstract materialism of natural science, a materialism that excludes the historical process, are immediately evident from the abstract and ideological conceptions of its spokesmen, whenever they venture beyond the bounds of their own speciality.'

43. *Economic and Philosophic Manuscripts of 1844*, pp. 109–11.

PART III

1. Marx, *Capital*, vol. 1 (Harmondsworth: Penguin Books, 1976) p. 133.

2. Ibid. p. 132.

3. Ibid. p. 492.

4. Ibid. p. 458.

5. Ibid. pp. 489–90.

6. Ibid. p. 494.

7. Ibid. p. 497.

8. Ibid. pp. 502–3.

9. Marx, *Grundrisse* (Harmondsworth: Penguin Books, 1973) p. 703.

10. Ibid. p. 719.

11. J. M. Clark, *Studies in the Economics of Overhead Costs* (London: University of Chicago Press, 1923).

12. E. Schmalenbach, A lecture was given by him 31 May 1928 headed: 'Die Betriebswirtschaftslehre an der Schwelle der neuen Wirtschaftsverfassung' (The Science of Management on the

Threshold of the New Economic Structure), in *Zeitschrift für Handelswiss. Forschung*, 32. Jahrg, Heft V.

13. Marx, *Capital*, vol. 3, p. 929.
14. V. I. Lenin, 'Imperialism, the Highest Stage of Capitalism', *Selected Works*, vol. 5 (Lawrence & Wishart, 1944) p. 72.
15. Frederick Winslow Taylor, *A Piece Rate System, being a step toward a Partial Solution of the Labor Problem*, a lecture given in 1895 to the American Society of Mechanical Engineers.
16. Harry Braverman, *Labor and Monopoly Capital: The Degradation of Work in the Twentieth Century* (New York: Monthly Review Press, 1974).
17. The Towne – Halsey Plan was published in the *Periodical of the Mechanical Engineers* of 1891.
18. F. W. Taylor, *Scientific Management* including: *Shop Management* (of 1903) and *The Principles of Scientific Management* (of 1911) (New York: Norton, 1967).
19. F. W. Taylor, *On the Art of Cutting Metals*, an address made to the Annual Meeting and published under the auspices of the American Society of Mechanical Engineers, 1906.
20. Frank B. Gilbreth, *Motion Study* (New York, 1911); and *Bricklaying System* (Chicago, n. d.).
21. Marx, *Capital*, vol. 1, pp. 548–9.
22. Taylor, *Shop Management*.
23. Marx, *Capital*, vol. 1, p. 451.
24. Gustavus F. Swift, the first man who used mechanised assembly-line work for meat-packing in Chicago in the 1880s by organising an overhead rail with hooks on which hung the carcasses of pigs or beef; men stood beneath the rail and each cut his agreed portion for packing while the overhead transfer moved on. The speed was compulsorily regulated. He finished by conquering the world market for pork.
25. Henry Ford, *My Life and Work*, 2nd edn (London, 1928).
26. Taylor, *Shop Management*.
27. Ford, op. cit. p. 72.
28. Marx, *Capital*, vol. 1, p. 502.
29. Marx, *Grundrisse* (Harmondsworth: Penguin Books (Pelican Marx Library), 1973) p. 159.
30. Marx – Engels, *Selected Correspondence* (London: Lawrence & Wishart, 1934) p. 246.
31. Marx, *Grundrisse*, pp. 172–3.
32. Marx, *Capital*, vol. 1, p. 166.
33. Harry Braverman, *Labor and Monopoly Capital: The Degradation of Work in the Twentieth Century* (New York: Monthly Review Press,

1974). I refer the reader to this outstanding study. See also M. J. E. Cooley, *Computer-Aided Design: Its Nature and Implications* (Richmond: Amalgamated Union of Engineering Workers (Technical and Supervisory Section), 1972).

34. Marx, *Grundrisse*, p. 717.
35. Marx, *Capital*, vol. 1, p. 284.
36. Robert Boguslaw, 'Operating Units', in *Design of Jobs*, ed. Louis E. Davis and James C. Taylor (Harmondsworth: Penguin Books, 1972).
37. Marx, *Capital*, vol. 1, p. 447.
38. Ibid. p. 495.
39. Ibid. p. 499.
40. Ibid. p. 545.
41. Ibid. p. 799.
42. Cf. M. J. E. Cooley, 'Contradictions of Science and Technology in the Productive Process', in *The Political Economy of Science*, ed. Hilary and Steven Rose (London: Macmillan, 1976).
43. Ernst Bloch, *Das Prinzip Hoffnung* (Frankfurt/Main: Suhrkamp, 1959) pp. 786 ff.
44. David E. Lilienthal, *TVA, Tennessee Valley Authority: Democracy on the March* (Harmondsworth: Penguin Books (Penguin Special (s 151)), 1944) p. 17.
45. Jack Westoby, 'Whose Trees? in *The New Scientist* (12 Aug 1976), and in *China Now* (Society for Anglo-Chinese Understanding (S.A.C.U.), Feb 1977).
46. Stalin's 'Plan for the Remaking of Nature', in *Soviet News* (London: Press Dept, Soviet Embassy, 1948) nos 2099, 2100.
47. Cf. Stalin, Dialectical and Historical Materialism', in *The History of the Communist Party of the Soviet Union (Bolsheviks)*, 1st edn (1938) pp. 105 ff.
48. This indebtedness of science to technology rather than the reverse is argued to have been a widespread rule throughout our industrial past, especially in the age of the industrial revolution but also prior to it in the very rise of modern science, as much as in the present, by a German scientist H. D. Dombrowski in his paper, *Physikalische Grundlagen und Analysen technischer Systeme* (Physical Foundations and Analyses of Technological Systems) (forthcoming).

PART IV

1. Todor Pavlov, *Die Widespiegelungstheorie* (The Theory of Reflexion) (Berlin: V.E.B. Deutscher Verlag der Wissenschaften, 1973).

2. Alexeyev Nikolayev Leontyev, *Probleme der Entwicklung des Psychis-chen* (Problems of the Development of the Human Psyche) (Frankfurt am Main: Athenäum Fischer Taschenbuch Verlag, 1973).

3. *Marxistisch-Leninistisches Wörterbuch der Philosophie*, ed. G. Klaus and M. Buhr (Hamburg: Rowohlt, 1972).

4. Bodo von Greiff, *Gesellschaftsform und Erkenntnisform, Zum Zusam-menhang von wissenschaftlicher Erfahrung und Gesellschaftlicher En-twicklung* (*Societal Form and Form of Cognition, Scientific Experience and Social Development in their Interconnection*) (Frankfurt am Main and New York: Campus-Verlag, 1976).

5. Winfried Hacker, *Allgemeine Arbeits- und Ingenieurpsychologie* (Gen-eral Psychology of Labour and Engineering) (Berlin: V.E.B. Deutscher Verlag der Wissenschaften, 1973).

6. Marx, *Capital*, vol. 1, p. 174 (footnote).

7. Ibid. p. 125.

8. K. Kautsky, *Theorien über den Mehrwert* (*Theories on Surplus-Value*), 3 vols (Berlin, 1905–1910). English part-edition by E. Burns (London: Lawrence & Wishart, 1951).

9. Marx, *Capital*, vol. 1, postface to 2nd edn, p. 97.

10. Ibid. p. 744.

11. K. Marx and F. Engels, *The German Ideology*. The passage I quote was crossed out by Marx in the manuscript and not printed in the English edition I possess: the one published in The Marxist-Leninist Library by Lawrence & Wishart, 1940.

12. Marx, *Capital*, vol. 1, preface to 1st edn, p. 92.

13. Ibid. p. 90.

BOOKS BY ALFRED SOHN-RETHEL

1. *Geistige und Körperliche Arbeit, Zur Theorie der gesellschaftlichen Synthesis*, 1st ed. (Frankfurt am Main: Suhrkamp Verlag, 1970); 2nd ed. (revised and enlarged) 1972, Edition Suhrkamp 555 (translated into Danish, Japanese and Italian).
2. *Warenform und Denkform*, Aufsätze (Frankfurt/Wien: Europäische Verlagsanstalt, 1971).
3. *Materialistische Erkenntniskritik und Vergesellschaftung der Arbeit*. Internationale Marxistische Diskussion 19 (Berlin: Merwe Verlag, 1971).
4. *Die ökonomische Doppelnatur des Spätkapitalismus* (Darmstadt und Neuwied: Luchterhand Verlag, 1972).
5. *Ökonomie und Klassenstruktur des deutschen Faschismus, Aufzeichnungen und Analysen*. (Frankfurt am Main: Edition Suhrkamp 630, 1973). (translated into Danish and Dutch)

ARTICLES IN ENGLISH BY ALFRED SOHN-RETHEL

1. 'The Advocacy of Materialism', *The Modern Quarterly*, New Series, vol. 3, no. 1, Winter 1947/8 (Lawrence & Wishart).
2. 'Historical-Materialist Theory of Knowledge', *Marxism Today*, Apr 1965 (Lawrence & Wishart).
3. 'Imperialism, the Era of Dual Economics. Suggestions for a Marxist Critique of "Scientific Management"', *Praxis* (Zagreb, Yugoslavia) no. 1/2, 1969.
4. 'Mental and Manual Labour in Marxism', in *Situating Marx*, ed. Paul Walton and Stuart Hall (Human Context Books by the Chaucer Publishing Co. Ltd, 1972).
5. 'Intellectual and Manual Labour', *Radical Philosophy* 6. Winter 1973 (Published by the Radical Philosophy Group).
6. 'Science as Alienated Consciousness', *Radical Science Journal*, no. 2/3, 1975. 9 (Poland Street, London).
7. 'The Dual Economics of Transition', *CSE Pamphlet*, no. 1, 1976 (Conference of Socialist Economists, 21 Theobalds Road, London).

Index

abstract nature 57
Accademia del Disegno 114
Adorno, T. W. xi
Aegean 98, 100
Ahmes 90, 91, 102
alienation 4, 47, 61, 67–8, 71, 72
Althusser, Louis xii, 20
Anaximander 72, 100
Apollonius 103
Arabs 91, 108, 109
Archimedes 103
Aristotle 60, 193
automation 172–5
automatism (postulate of) 121, 122, 141, 154
automaton 121

Babylon 25, 99
Bacon, Roger 108
Bebel, August xii
Benedetti 114
Benjamin, Walter xi, xiii
Bernal, J. D. xiv
Bloch, Ernst xi, xiii, 181
Boguslaw, Robert 173
bourgeois science 132–5, 178–90
Bradwardine, Thomas 108
Braverman, Harry 148
Bronze Age 25, 88–94, 95, 99, 101
Byzantium 107, 109

Cantor, Moritz 102, 108, 114
Cardano 116
Cassirer, Ernst xiii
Cataldi, P. A. 114
Cavalieri 116
Clark, J. M. 144
Constantinople 113, 124
Cornford, Francis Macdonald 71
Crusades 109

Danes 107
Descartes 14, 77, 123, 126
Domesday Book 106
Duns Scotus 108

Durer, Albrecht 113–16

economics of time 149, 161, 165, 167, 172, 173
Edward III 109
Egypt 22, 25, 88–93, 103–9
emancipation 175–8
empiricism 26, 193–4
enclosure acts 109
equivalence 6, 49, 50
Erastosthenes 103
Etruscans 94
Euclid 103, 109, 114, 116, 127
exchange equation 6, 46–7, 48, 98

false consciousness 21, 72, 194–201
Farrington, Benjamin 99
Ferrari 116
feudalism 105–9
Flanders 107, 109
Florence 107, 114
Ford, Henry 158–61, 172
Frederic II 109
French Revolution 14, 36
Fromm, Erich 42 n.

Galileo 14, 17, 74, 111, 114, 122–32, 190
Gilbreth, Frank 155
Greece xiv, 25, 28, 58, 59, 78, 86, 94–103, 108, 109
Greek philosophy 22, 28, 66, 88, 190
Greiff, Bodo von 192
Grosseteste, Robert 107, 108

Hacker, Winfried 193
Halsey, F. A. 149
Heath, Sir Thomas 102
Hegel 14–17, 20, 65–8, 133, 134, 200
Heidegger xiii
Heraclitus 19, 65
Herodotus 90, 100
Heron 103
Hilton, Rodney 107
Hitler-Germany 164
Hobbes 123

Hollerith 173
Horkheimer, Max xi
Hume, David 46

Indian mathematics 91, 108, 109
inertial motion 123-32
Ionia 65, 98-100
Iron Age 25, 78, 94
Italy 98, 107, 109, 162, 163

Kant, Immanuel 7, 13-17, 21, 30, 35-
9, 74, 77, 129, 193
Kautsky, Karl 197
Kepler, Johannes 114
Korean War 164
Koyré, Alexander xiii, 125, 126, 127
Kracauer, Siegfried xi
Kroton 48
Kugelmann 50, 166

Lenin xii, 144, 147
Leonardo da Pisa 108
Leontyev, Alexeyev Nikolayev 190
Lilienthal, David E. 181
Lukacs, Georg xi, 193
Lysenko, T. D. 183

Mao Tse-tung 183
Marcuse, Herbert xi, 42
Mesopotamia 22, 103
Midas, King 28
Middle Ages 129
Miletus 99, 100
Monte, G. del 114
Morgan, Lewis 95

Needham, Joseph 91
Newton, Isaac 17, 74, 124, 126, 190
Nietzsche, Friedrich 39
Nile 88, 90, 91
Nuremberg 113, 116

Occam, William 108
Olschki, Leonardo 114
Oschinsky, Dorothea 107
Oxford 108

Paris, School of 108
Parker, Richard A. 91
Parmenides 19, 65, 66, 68, 71
Pavlov, Todor 189
Petty, William 13, 192
Phoenicians 94, 100
Pirckheimer, Willibald 113
Pirelli strike 162

Plato 63, 103
Pythagoras 19, 47, 65

real abstraction 20, 21, 28, 57, 60-7, 69,
70, 72, 76
Reich, Wilhelm 42 n.
reification 47, 99
Renaissance 110, 129
Rhind Papyrus 90
Rhodes, Cecil 147
Ricardo, David 13, 14, 36, 195
Russell, Bertrand 41, 127, 130, 131

Samos 48
Schmalenbach, Eugen 144
Schmidt, Alfred 3
Schott, Siegfried 91
Second Nature 28, 45, 57, 61, 73, 75,
103, 110, 118, 175, 178, 183
Seidel, Alfred xii
slave labour 28, 52, 77, 78, 86, 96, 98,
104, 105
Smith, Adam 13, 14, 35, 36, 195
Smith, D. F. 102
Socrates 64
Solon 72
Sophocles 71
Stalin, Joseph 181, 183
Swift of Chicago 158

Tartaglia, Nicolo 114, 116
Taylor, Frederick Winslow 147-61,
165, 170, 171
Taylorism 149 ff., 159, 160, 165, 170
Tennessee Valley Authority 181, 184
Thales 60, 72, 99, 100
Thomson, George xii, 40, 71, 95, 98, 100
Toller, Ernst xii
Torricelli 126
Towne, H. R. 149
Turks 113, 124

van der Will, Wilfried xiv
Venice 113, 116
Vietnam War 164

Weber, Alfred xiii
Weber, Max xiii
Werner, Johann 114
Westoby, Jack 182
wool trade 109

Zeno 54
Zienau, Sigurd xiv